More or Less

BRITANNICA
Mathematics in Context

Number

HOLT, RINEHART AND WINSTON

Mathematics in Context is a comprehensive curriculum for the middle grades. It was developed in 1991 through 1997 in collaboration with the Wisconsin Center for Education Research, School of Education, University of Wisconsin-Madison and the Freudenthal Institute at the University of Utrecht, The Netherlands, with the support of the National Science Foundation Grant No. 9054928.

The revision of the curriculum was carried out in 2003 through 2005, with the support of the National Science Foundation Grant No. ESI 0137414.

National Science Foundation

Opinions expressed are those of the authors and not necessarily those of the Foundation.

Keijzer, R.; van den Heuvel-Panhuizen, M.; Abels, M.; Wijers, M.; Shew, J. A.; Brinker, L.; Pligge, M. A.; Shafer, M.; and Brendefur, J. (2006). *More or less.* In Wisconsin Center for Education Research & Freudenthal Institute (Eds.), *Mathematics in context.* Chicago: Encyclopædia Britannica, Inc.

The Teacher's Guide for this unit was prepared by David C. Webb, Teri Hedges, Mieke Abels, and Dédé de Haan.

2006 Printed by Holt, Rinehart and Winston

ISBN 0-03-039807-X

4 5 6 073 09 08 07

The *Mathematics in Context* Development Team

Development 1991–1997

The initial version of *More or Less* was developed by Ronald Keijzer, Marja van den Heuvel-Panhuizen, and Monica Wijers. It was adapted for use in American schools by Julia Shew, Laura Brinker, Margaret A. Pligge, Mary Shafer, and Jonathan Brendefur.

Wisconsin Center for Education Research Staff

Thomas A. Romberg
Director

Joan Daniels Pedro
Assistant to the Director

Gail Burrill
Coordinator

Margaret R. Meyer
Coordinator

Freudenthal Institute Staff

Jan de Lange
Director

Els Feijs
Coordinator

Martin van Reeuwijk
Coordinator

Project Staff

Jonathan Brendefur
Laura Brinker
James Browne
Jack Burrill
Rose Byrd
Peter Christiansen
Barbara Clarke
Doug Clarke
Beth R. Cole
Fae Dremock
Mary Ann Fix

Sherian Foster
James A. Middleton
Jasmina Milinkovic
Margaret A. Pligge
Mary C. Shafer
Julia A. Shew
Aaron N. Simon
Marvin Smith
Stephanie Z. Smith
Mary S. Spence

Mieke Abels
Nina Boswinkel
Frans van Galen
Koeno Gravemeijer
Marja van den Heuvel-Panhuizen
Jan Auke de Jong
Vincent Jonker
Ronald Keijzer
Martin Kindt

Jansie Niehaus
Nanda Querelle
Anton Roodhardt
Leen Streefland
Adri Treffers
Monica Wijers
Astrid de Wild

Revision 2003–2005

The revised version of *More or Less* was developed by Mieke Abels and Monica Wijers. It was adapted for use in American schools by Margaret A. Pligge.

Wisconsin Center for Education Research Staff

Thomas A. Romberg
Director

David C. Webb
Coordinator

Gail Burrill
Editorial Coordinator

Margaret A. Pligge
Editorial Coordinator

Freudenthal Institute Staff

Jan de Lange
Director

Truus Dekker
Coordinator

Mieke Abels
Content Coordinator

Monica Wijers
Content Coordinator

Project Staff

Sarah Ailts
Beth R. Cole
Erin Hazlett
Teri Hedges
Karen Hoiberg
Carrie Johnson
Jean Krusi
Elaine McGrath

Margaret R. Meyer
Anne Park
Bryna Rappaport
Kathleen A. Steele
Ana C. Stephens
Candace Ulmer
Jill Vettrus

Arthur Bakker
Peter Boon
Els Feijs
Dédé de Haan
Martin Kindt

Nathalie Kuijpers
Huub Nilwik
Sonia Palha
Nanda Querelle
Martin van Reeuwijk

Cover photo credits: (left to right) © Comstock Images; © Corbis; © Getty Images

Illustrations
xviii (all) Christine McCabe/©Encyclopædia Britannica, Inc.; **5, 18** (left), **19** (top), **20** Christine McCabe/© Encyclopædia Britannica, Inc.; **22** Holly Cooper-Olds; **27** © Encyclopædia Britannica, Inc.; **30** Christine McCabe/© Encyclopædia Britannica, Inc.

Photographs
xi (all) Sam Dudgeon/HRW Photo; **xvii** PhotoDisc/Getty Images; **xviii** Victoria Smith/HRW; **1–5** Sam Dudgeon/HRW Photo; **6** © PhotoDisc/Getty Images; **12** (left to right) John Langford/HRW; © Ryan McVay/PhotoDisc/Getty Images; Don Couch/HRW Photo; **13** John Langford/HRW; **17** © Ryan McVay/PhotoDisc/Getty Images; Don Couch/HRW Photo; **19** Sam Dudgeon/HRW Photo; **26, 27** Comstock Images/Alamy; **28, 29** ©1998 Image Farm Inc.

Contents

Dear Teacher,

Welcome! *Mathematics in Context* is designed to reflect the National Council of Teachers of Mathematics *Principles and Standards for School Mathematics* and the results of decades of classroom-based education research. *Mathematics in Context* was designed according to the principles of Realistic Mathematics Education, a Dutch approach to mathematics teaching and learning. In this approach mathematical content is grounded in a variety of realistic contexts in order to promote student engagement and understanding of mathematics. The term *realistic* is meant to convey the idea that the contexts and mathematics can be made "real in your mind." Rather than relying on you to explain and demonstrate generalized definitions, rules, or algorithms, students investigate questions directly related to a particular context and develop mathematical understanding and meaning from that context.

The curriculum encompasses nine units per grade level. *More or Less* is designed to be the third unit in the Number Strand, but it also lends itself to independent use—to connect and expand students' knowledge of fractions, decimals, and percents.

In addition to the Teacher's Guides and Student Books, *Mathematics in Context* offers the following components that will inform and support your teaching:

- ***Teacher Implementation Guide*, which provides an overview of the complete system and resources for program implementation.**
- ***Number Tools* and *Algebra Tools*, which are black-line master resources that serve as review sheets or practice pages to support the development of basic skills and extend student understanding of concepts developed in number and algebra units.**
- ***Mathematics in Context Online*, which is a rich, balanced resource for teachers, students, and parents looking for additional information, activities, tools, and support to further students' mathematical understanding and achievements.**

Thank you for choosing *Mathematics in Context*. We wish you success and inspiration!

Sincerely,

The Mathematics in Context Development Team

More or Less and the NCTM Principles and Standards for School Mathematics for Grades 6–8

The process standards of Problem Solving, Reasoning and Proof, Communication, Connections, and Representation are addressed across all *Mathematics in Context* units.

In addition, this unit specifically addresses the following PSSM content standards and expectations:

Number and Operations

In grades 6–8 all students should:

- work flexibly with fractions, decimals, and percents to solve problems;
- compare and order fractions, decimals, and percents efficiently;
- develop meaning for percents greater than 100 and less than 1;
- understand and use ratios and proportions to represent quantitative relationships;
- understand the meaning and effects of arithmetic operations with fractions, decimals, and integers;
- understand and use the inverse relationships of addition and subtraction, multiplication and division to simplify computations and solve problems;
- select appropriate methods and tools for computing with fractions and decimals from among mental computation, estimation, calculators or computers, and paper and pencil, depending on the situation, and apply the selected methods;
- develop and analyze algorithms for computing with fractions, decimals, and integers and develop fluency in their use;
- develop and use strategies to estimate the results of rational-number computations and judge the reasonableness of the results; and
- develop, analyze, and explain methods for solving problems involving proportions, such as scaling and finding equivalent ratios.

Measurement

In grades 6–8 all students should:

- select and apply techniques and tools to accurately find length, area, volume, and angle measures to appropriate levels of precision and
- solve problems involving scale factors, using ratio and proportion.

Math in the Unit

This is the third Number unit in grade 6. *More or Less* helps students formalize, connect, and expand their knowledge of fractions, decimals, and percents in number and geometry contexts. Problems involving the multiplication of decimals and percents are introduced. In *More or Less,* students extend their understanding of the connections between fractions and decimals and explore connections between these types of rational numbers and percents.

Students use benchmark fractions to find percents and discounts and use one-step multiplication calculations to compute sale prices and prices that include tax. Arrow strings as developed in the Algebra Strand are used to find the dimensions of enlarged or reduced photocopies and to connect the percent decrease and increase to multiplication.

For example, the arrow string below describes a reduction to 80%.

original length $\xrightarrow{\times 0.8}$ reduced length

Models

In this unit the number models are reviewed. The double number line and the percent bar are especially used to give visual support.

The *double number line* is a number tool that is used throughout the *Mathematics in Context* curriculum to solve problems involving fractions, decimals, percents, and whole numbers. In this unit, students use the double number line to calculate the cost of produce. Like the ratio table number model, the double number line generates equivalent ratios. In the case of pricing produce, students use this feature to multiply the price per kilogram and label regularly spaced marks on the double number line. If, for example, 1 kg of apples cost $2.40, students can estimate a cost at or near 1.75 kg by first doubling $2.40 to determine what 2 kg will cost. Then, students repeatedly find the number halfway between two numbers:

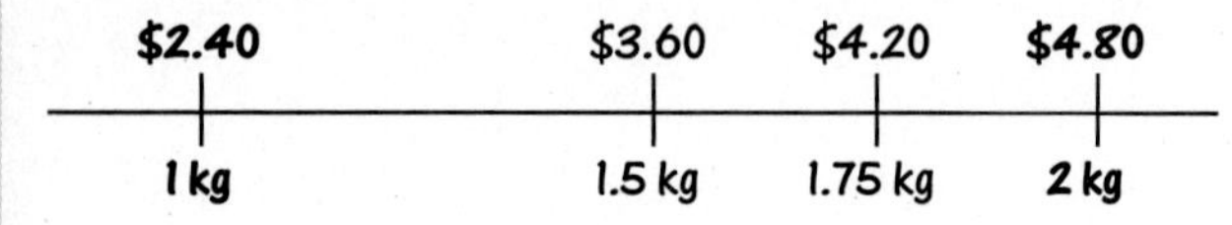

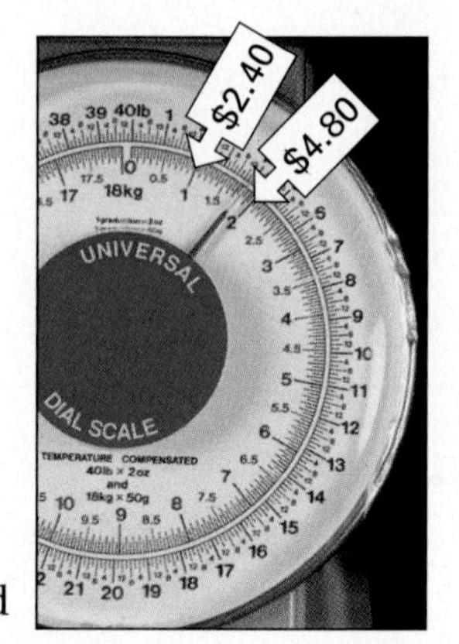

The double number line is revisited in the context of a supermarket produce department. Students use the scale and the price per kilogram to estimate and calculate the cost of produce.

The *percent bar* is a model that is developed in the *Mathematics in Context* curriculum to represent and make sense of calculations and problems involving percents. With a scale for the percent across the bottom and a scale for the price along the top, students use their knowledge of benchmark fractions and percents to calculate percent decrease or increase. Because the percent bar is a visual model, students reason and justify calculations by relating the model to the context of the problem.

The percent bar helps students connect fractions and percents.

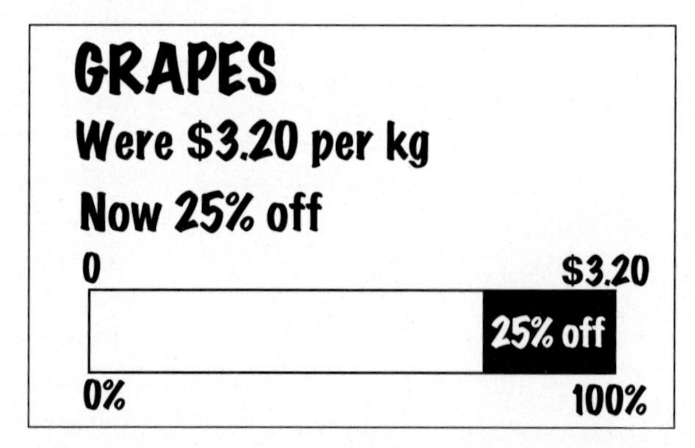

Finally, to calculate a percent increase or decrease there are many tools students can use: a ratio table, a percent bar, a double number line, or arrow strings.

The skills and concepts developed in *More or Less* are reinforced by the activities in *Number Tools*, Section A.

On the *Mathematics in Context* Web site (http://my.hrw.com) applets for extra practice can be found (for example, Estimate, the Jump Jump Game, etc);

When students have finished the unit they:

- Develop number sense and a conceptual understanding of ratios:
  - use an estimation strategy to find the cost of produce, for example, by rounding decimals to whole numbers, by using benchmark fractions like halves or quarters and
  - use an exact calculation to find the cost of produce, for example, by changing the decimal numbers into fractions or by using a calculator.
- Develop number sense and a conceptual understanding of percents:
  - calculate the sale price of an item with a discount given as a percent or fraction;
  - start to use multiplication in percent decrease situations, for example, to find the sale price of an item with a discount given as a percent or fraction;
  - understand that increasing a price by a certain percent is the same as taking 100% plus that percent of the price; for example, increasing a price by 50% is the same as finding 150% of that price; and
  - start to use multiplication in situations of a percent increase, for example when finding the total price of an item sales tax included, or the dimensions of an enlarged picture.

- Develop number sense and a conceptual understanding of fractions, decimals, percents, and ratios:
  - multiply fractions and decimals;
  - understand and use benchmark fractions and their relation to ratios, percents and decimals;
  - use the relationship of ratios, percents, and decimals to solve problems; and
  - choose an appropriate model or tool to solve problems where fractions, decimals, percents, and ratios are involved (a ratio table, a percent bar, a double number line, arrow strings, a calculator).

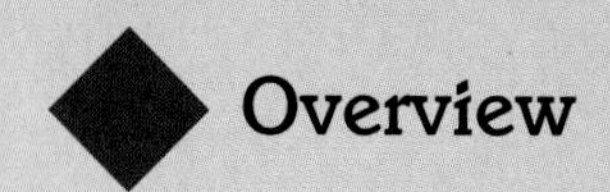

Number Strand: An Overview

Mathematical Content

The Number strand in *Mathematics in Context* emphasizes number sense, computations with number, and the ability to use number to better understand a situation. The broad category of number includes the concepts of magnitude, order, computation, relationships among numbers, and relationships among the various representations of number, such as fractions, decimals, and percents. In addition, ideas of ratio and proportion are developed gradually and are integrated with the other number representations. A theme that extends throughout the strand is using models as tools. Models are developed and used to help support student understanding of these concepts. The goals of the units within the Number strand are aligned with NCTM's *Principles and Standards for School Mathematics.*

Number Sense and Using Models as Tools

While the number sense theme is embedded in all the number units, this theme is emphasized in the additional resource, *Number Tools.* The activities in *Number Tools* reinforce students' understanding of ratios, fractions, decimals, and percents, and the connections between these representations. The using-models-as-tools theme is also embedded in every number unit.

Organization of the Number Strand

The Number strand has two major themes: develop and use models as tools and develop and use number sense. The units in the Number Strand are organized into two main substrands: *Rational Number* and *Number Theory.* The map illustrates the strand organization.

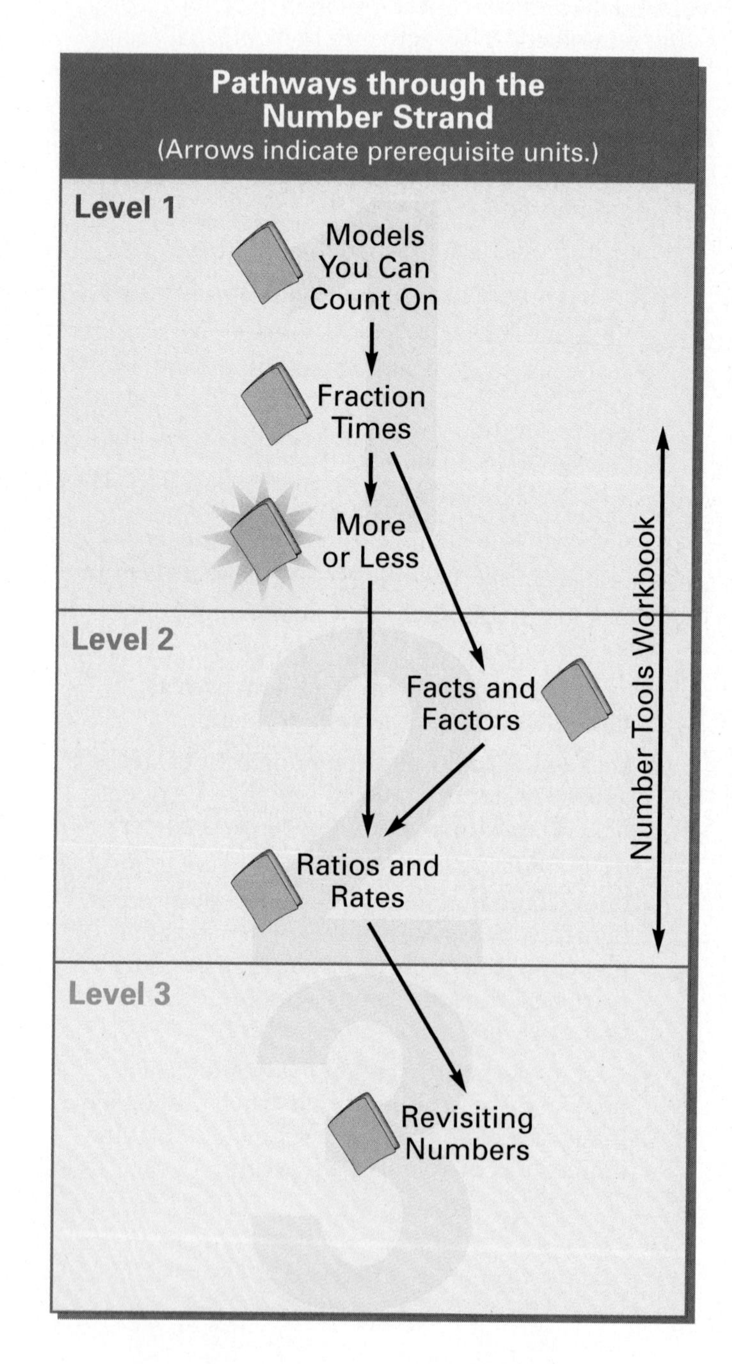

The *Mathematics in Context* Approach to Number, Using Models as Tools

Throughout the Number strand, models are important problem-solving tools because they develop students' understanding of fractions, decimals, percents, and ratios to make connections.

When a model is introduced, it is very closely related to a specific context; for example, in *Models You Can Count On*, students read gauges of a water tank and a coffee pot and they solve problems related to a download bar.

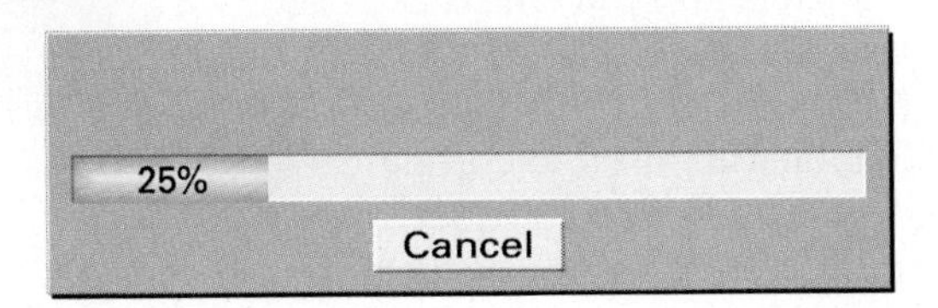

As students gain experience with the bar in different situations, it becomes more abstract and generalized, and can be used as a tool to solve fraction and percent problems in general. The fraction bar as well as the percent bar give the students visual support.

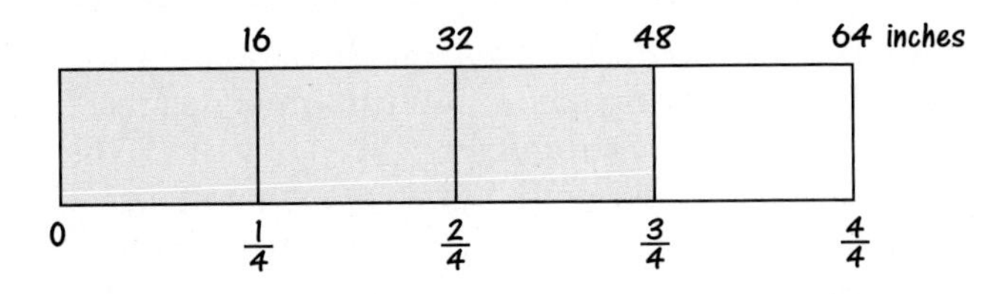

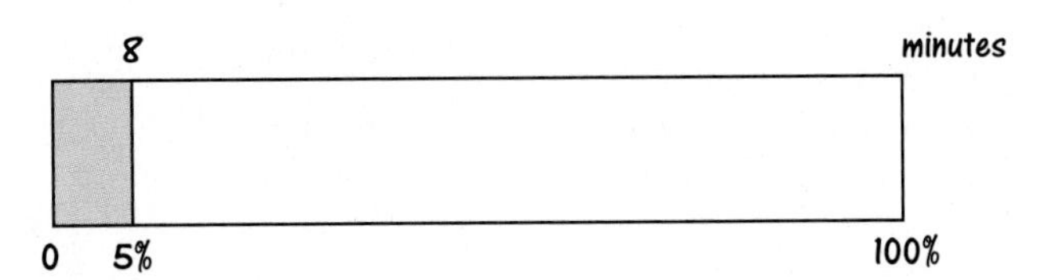

Double Number Line

Another model that students develop and use is the double number line. This model allows students to make accurate calculations and estimates as well, for all sorts of ratio problems, especially where real numbers are involved.

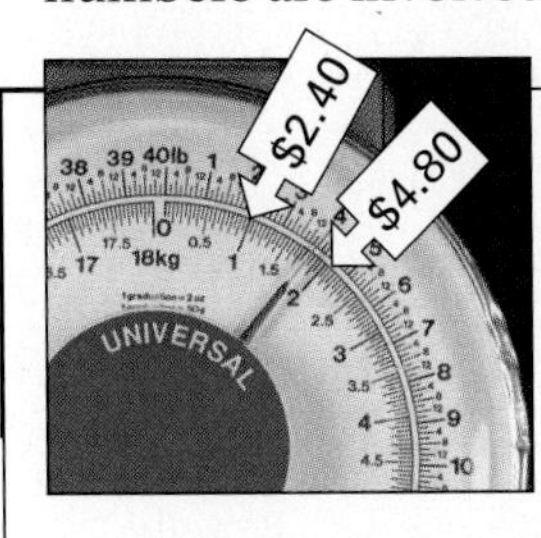

Pablo says, "That's almost 2 kg of apples."

Lia states, "That's about $1\frac{3}{4}$ kg of apples."

Pam suggests, "Use the scale as a double number line."

4. a. How will Pablo find the answer? What will Pablo estimate?

b. How will Lia calculate the answer? What will she estimate?

c. How will Pam use a double number line to estimate the cost of the apples?

The scale line on a map is also related to a double number line.

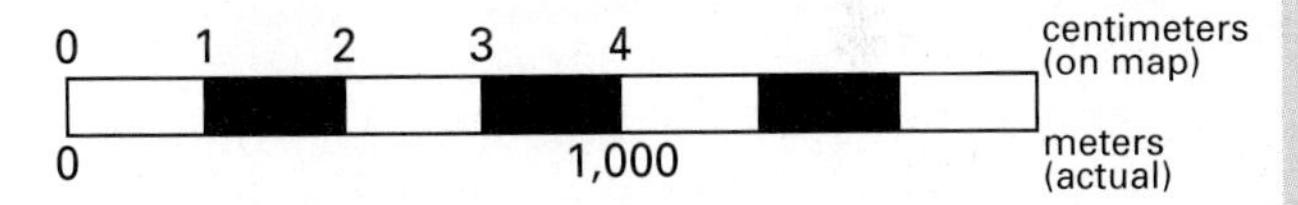

Number Line

The number line model is frequently used, and it is a general tool that applies to a wide range of problem contexts.

If students do not have a picture of a numbered number line, they can draw their own *empty number line* to make jumps by drawing curves between different lengths.

A number line is used to find the sum of two decimal numbers.

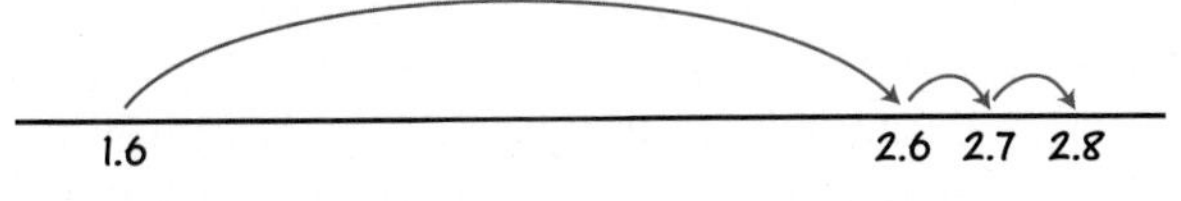

A jump of one and two jumps of 0.1 together make 1.2, so 1.6 + 1.2 = 2.8.

Note that on a single number line, fractions and decimals are seen as numbers—locations on number lines—and not as parts of wholes or operators.

Ratio Table

The difference between a ratio table and a double number line is that on a number line, the order of the numbers is fixed, whereas in a ratio table the numbers in the columns can be placed in any order that fits the calculation best.

Minutes	10	20	80	5	15	...
Miles	$\frac{1}{2}$	1	4	$\frac{1}{4}$	$\frac{3}{4}$	$4\frac{3}{4}$

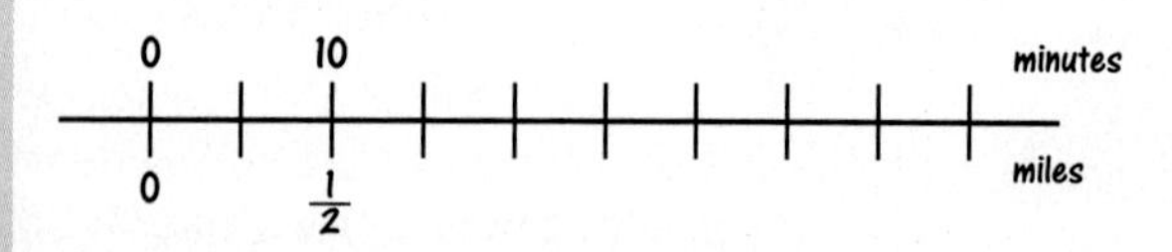

When necessary, students can draw on their prior experience with specific and generalized models to make challenging problems more accessible. They are free to choose any model that they want to use to solve problems. Some students may prefer a bar model or a double number line because they give visual support, while other students may prefer a ratio table.

The *Mathematics in Context* Approach to Number, Number Sense

The Number strand gives students ample opportunity to develop computation, estimation, and number sense skills and to decide when to use each technique. In *Mathematics in Context,* it is more important for students to understand computation and use their own accurate computation strategies than it is for them to use formal algorithms that they don't understand. Because number concepts are an integral part of every unit in the curriculum—not just those in the Number strand—every unit extends students' understanding of number.

Rational Number

The first unit in the Number strand, *Models You Can Count On,* builds on students' informal knowledge of ratios, part-whole relationships and benchmark percents. The unit emphasizes number models that can be used to support computation and develop students' number sense. For example, the ratio table is introduced with whole number ratios, and students develop strategies to generate equivalent ratios in the table.

These strategies are made explicit: adding, times 10, doubling, subtracting, multiplying, halving. Students informally add, multiply, and divide benchmark fractions. The context of money and the number line offer the opportunity to reinforce computations with decimal numbers.

The second unit in the Number strand, *Fraction Times,* makes connections and builds on the models, skills, and concepts that are developed in the unit *Models You Can Count On.*

Fraction Times further develops and extends students' understanding of relationships between fractions, decimals, and percents. Bar models and pie charts are used to make connections between fractions and percents. Bars or ratio tables are used to compare, informally add and subtract, and simplify fractions. The context of money is chosen to multiply whole numbers with decimals and to change fractions into decimals and decimals into fractions. When students calculate a fraction of a fraction by using fractions of whole numbers, students informally multiply fractions. Some of the operations with fractions are formalized.

In *More or Less,* students formalize, connect, and expand their knowledge of fractions, decimals, and percents in number and geometry contexts. Problems involving the multiplication of decimals and percents are introduced.
Students use benchmark fractions to find percents and discounts. They use one-step multiplication calculations to compute sale price and prices that include tax. They also use percents in a geometric context to find the dimensions of enlarged or reduced photocopies and then connect the percent increase to multiplication.

The unit *Facts and Factors* revisits the operations with fractions that were not formalized in the unit *Fraction Times.* This unit is a unit in the Number Theory substrand. The area model is developed and used to increase students' understanding of how to multiply fractions and mixed numbers.

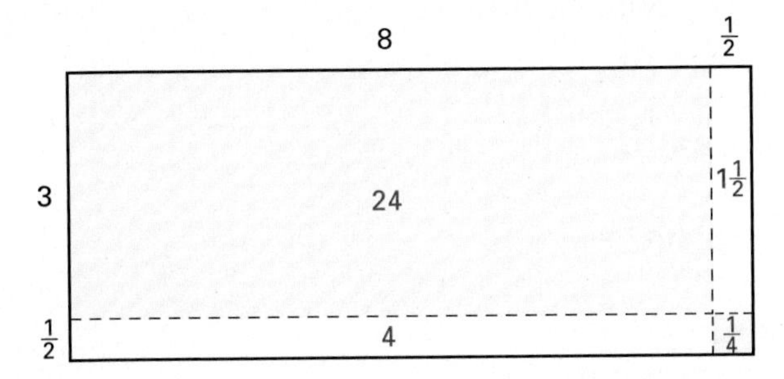

While *More or Less* extends students' understanding of the connections between fractions and decimals, the unit *Ratios and Rates* focuses on the connections between these types of rational numbers and percents. It relates ratios to fractions, decimals, and percents and introduces students to ratio as a single number. The use of number tools from earlier units is revisited. The double number line is revisited in the context of scale lines on a map. The ratio table is another model that is used in the context of scale. *Ratios and Rates* extends students' understanding of ratio. The use of ratio tables helps students understand that ratios and rates are also averages. When students start to compare ratios, the terms *relative comparison* and *absolute comparison* are introduced, and students discover the value of comparing ratios as opposed to looking only at absolute amounts. In realistic situations, students investigate part-part ratios and part-whole ratios.

The final unit of the Number strand, *Revisiting Numbers,* integrates concepts from both substrands. Rational number ideas are reviewed, extended, and formalized. This unit builds on experiences with the unit *Ratios and Rates* to further explore rates. In the context of speed, students use ratio tables to calculate rates and change units. Students solve context problems where operations (multiplication and division) with fractions and mixed numbers are involved. They use these experiences to solve "bare" problems by thinking of a context that fits the bare problem. Supported by the context and the models they can count on (a double number line, a ratio table, and the area model), students develop their own strategies to solve all types of problems.

Number Theory

The Level 2 number unit, *Facts and Factors,* helps students to get a better understanding of the base-ten number system. Students study number notation, the naming of large numbers, powers of ten, powers of two, and exponential notation. Students investigate how a calculator shows very large numbers and make connections with the product of a number and a power of ten: the scientific notation.

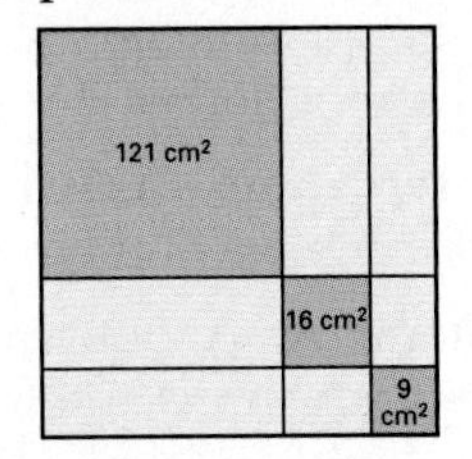

They use scientific notation only in a "passive" way. Very small numbers are investigated in the number unit *Revisiting Numbers.* Students use several strategies, including upside-down arithmetic trees, to factor composite numbers into their prime factors. Using the sides and area of a square of graph paper, the relationship between squares and square roots is explored. This unit expands students' understanding of rational and irrational numbers at an informal level.

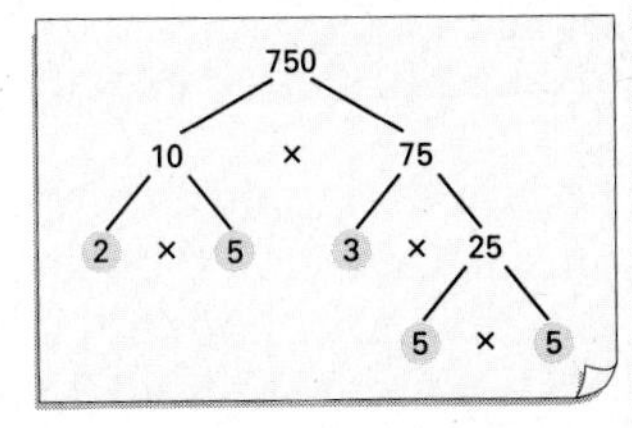

The unit *Revisiting Numbers* is the last unit in the Number strand. A conceptual understanding of natural numbers, whole numbers, integers, rational numbers, irrational numbers, and real numbers is developed. This unit builds on students' previous experience with numbers.

Investigations of relationships between operations and their inverses promote understanding of whole numbers, integers, and rational and irrational numbers. The calculator notation and the scientific notation for large numbers are reviewed from the unit *Facts and Factors* and extended with these notations for small numbers. Multiplication and division with positive and negative powers of ten are formalized. Supported by contexts and the area model, the commutative property, the distributive property, and the associative property are investigated and formalized.

Student Assessment in Mathematics in Context

As recommended by the NCTM *Principles and Standards for School Mathematics* and research on student learning, classroom assessment should be based on evidence drawn from several sources. An assessment plan for a *Mathematics in Context* unit may draw from the following overlapping sources:

- **observation—As students work individually or in groups, watch for evidence of their understanding of the mathematics.**
- **interactive responses—Listen closely to how students respond to your questions and to the responses of other students.**
- **products—Look for clarity and quality of thought in students' solutions to problems completed in class, for homework, extensions, projects, quizzes, and tests.**

Assessment Pyramid

When designing a comprehensive assessment program, the assessment tasks used should be distributed across the following three dimensions: mathematics content, levels of reasoning, and difficulty level. The Assessment Pyramid, based on Jan de Lange's theory of assessment, is a model used to suggest how items should be distributed across these three dimensions. Over time, assessment questions should "fill" the pyramid.

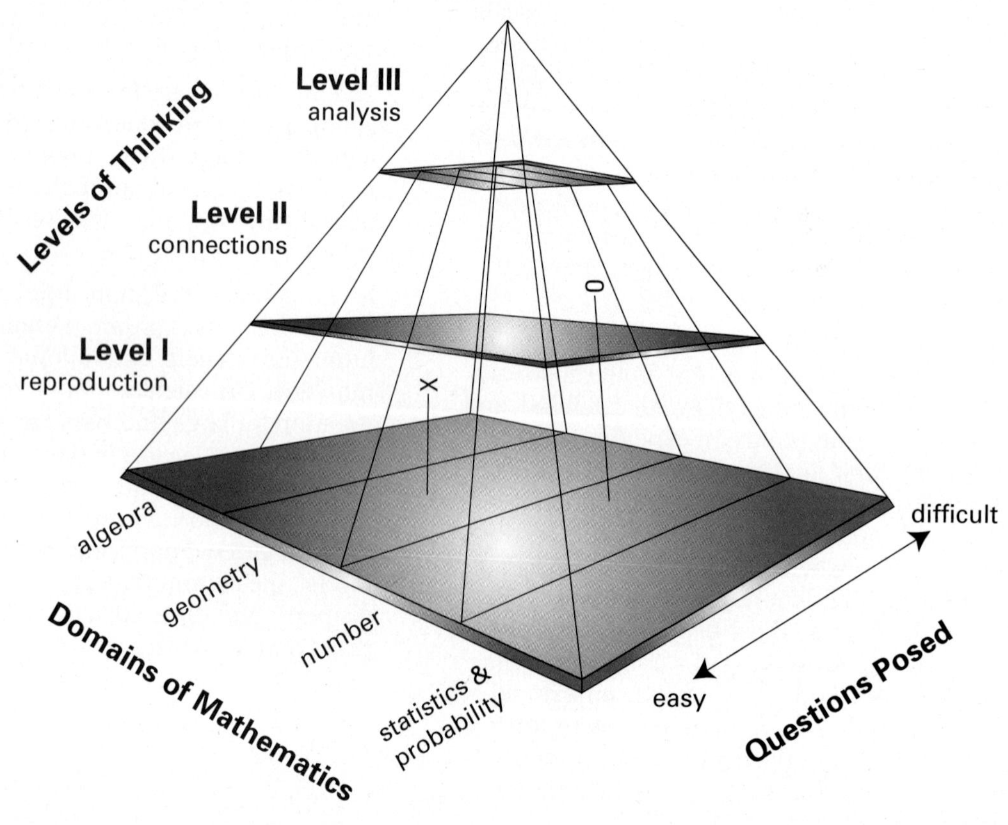

Levels of Reasoning

Level I questions typically address:

- recall of facts and definitions and
- use of technical skills, tools, and standard algorithms.

As shown in the pyramid, Level I questions are not necessarily easy. For example, Level I questions may involve complicated computation problems. In general, Level I questions assess basic knowledge and procedures that may have been emphasized during instruction. The format for this type of question is usually short answer, fill-in, or multiple choice. On a quiz or test, Level I questions closely resemble questions that are regularly found in a given unit, substituted with different numbers and/or contexts.

Level II questions require students to:

- integrate information;
- decide which mathematical models or tools to use for a given situation; and
- solve unfamiliar problems in a context, based on the mathematical content of the unit.

Level II questions are typically written to elicit short or extended responses. Students choose their own strategies, use a variety of mathematical models, and explain how they solved a problem.

Level III questions require students to:

- make their own assumptions to solve open-ended problems;
- analyze, interpret, synthesize, reflect; and
- develop one's own strategies or mathematical models.

Level II questions are always open-ended problems. Often, more than one answer is possible, and there is a wide variation in reasoning and explanations. There are limitations to the type of Level III problems that students can be reasonably expected to respond to on time-restricted tests.

The instructional decisions a teacher makes as he or she progresses through a unit may influence the level of reasoning required to solve problems. If a method of problem solving required to solve a Level III problem is repeatedly emphasized during instruction, the level of reasoning required to solve a Level II or III problem may be reduced to recall knowledge, or Level I reasoning. A student who does not master a specific algorithm during a unit but solves a problem correctly using his or her own invented strategy, may demonstrate higher-level reasoning than a student who memorizes and applies an algorithm.

The "volume" represented by each level of the Assessment Pyramid serves as a guideline for the distribution of problems and use of score points over the three reasoning levels.

These assessment design principles are used throughout *Mathematics in Context*. The Goals and Assessment charts that highlight ongoing assessment opportunities—on pages xiv and xv of each Teacher's Guide—are organized according to levels of reasoning.

In the Lesson Notes section of the Teacher's Guide, ongoing assessment opportunities are also shown in the Assessment Pyramid icon, located at the bottom of the Notes column.

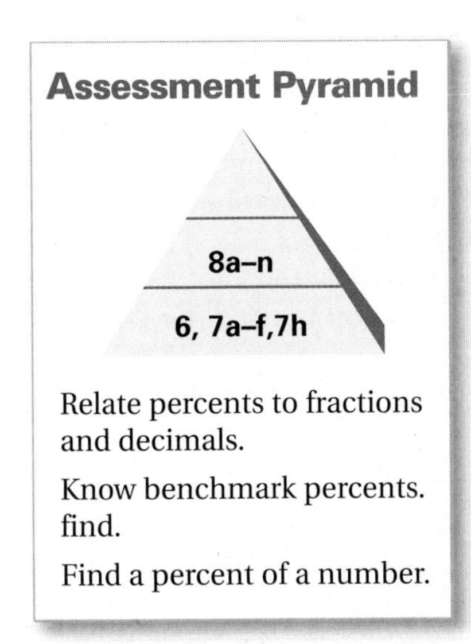

Goals and Assessment

In the *Mathematics in Context* curriculum, unit goals, organized according to levels of reasoning described in the Assessment Pyramid on page xiv, relate to the strand goals and the NCTM Principles and Standards for School Mathematics. The *Mathematics in Context* curriculum is designed to help students demonstrate their understanding of mathematics in each of the categories listed below. Ongoing assessment opportunities are also indicated on their respective pages throughout the Teacher's Guide by an Assessment Pyramid icon.

It is important to note that the attainment of goals in one category is not a prerequisite to the attainment of those in another category. In fact, students should progress simultaneously toward several goals in different categories. The Goals and Assessment table is designed to support preparation of an assessment plan.

	Goal	Ongoing Assessment Opportunities	Unit Assessment Opportunities
Level I: Conceptual and Procedural Knowledge	**1.** Use estimation strategies to multiply fractions and decimals	**Section A** p. 4, #9 p. 6, #16	**Quiz 1** #1ad **Test** #2ab
	2. Use number sense to multiply two decimal numbers	**Section A** p. 5, #14a–g p. 7, #18ab	**Quiz 1** #1bc **Quiz 2** #1ab **Test** #2ab
	3. Find a percent of a number	**Section B** p. 13, #7a–h **Section C** p. 22, #13	**Quiz 1** #2c **Quiz 2** #1b, 3c **Test** #3a
	4. Calculate discount and sale price	**Section C** p. 19, #5 p. 22, #14 **Section D** p. 28, #9c	**Quiz 1** #3ab **Quiz 2** #1b, 3c **Test** #1, 3b
	5. Know and use benchmark percents	**Section B** p. 13, #6 p. 14, #12a **Section C** p. 19, #6ab	**Quiz 1** #2abc, 3ab **Quiz 2** #2, 3ab **Test** #3abc

	Goal	Ongoing Assessment Opportunities	Unit Assessment Opportunities
Level II: Reasoning, Communicating, Thinking, and Making Connections	**6.** Relate percents to fractions and decimals	**Section B** p. 13, #8a-n p. 14, #9 **Section C** p. 19, #6ab **Section D** p. 27, #5ab p. 30, #14bc	**Quiz 1** #2abc **Quiz 2** #2, 3a
	7. Find an original price using the sale price and the percent discount	**Section C** p. 23, #18 p. 25, CYW #5 p. 29, #10b	**Test** #5ab
	8. Develop number sense	**Section A** p. 4, #9 p. 6, #15 **Section B** p. 14, #11 p. 15, #13a-e	**Quiz 1** #3b **Quiz 2** #1a **Test** #3c, 5b

	Goal	Ongoing Assessment Opportunities	Unit Assessment Opportunities
Level III: Modeling, Generalizing, and Non-Routine, Problem Solving	**9.** Understand common misconceptions of percent increase and decrease	**Section C** p. 22, #15ab p. 25, For Further Reflection	
	10. Explore use of percents as operators (use 1.5 to find a 50% increase)	**Section D** p. 29, #10a p. 30, #17	
	11. Explore multiplicative increase and decrease (e.g., compound interest)	**Section D** p. 27, #3abc p. 31, #21	**Test** #4

Materials Preparation

The following items are the necessary materials and resources to be used by the teacher and students throughout the unit. For further details, see the Section Overviews and the Materials sections of the Hints and Comments column of each teacher page. Note: Some contexts and problems can be enhanced through the use of optional materials. These optional materials are listed in the corresponding Hints and Comments section.

Student Resources

Quantities listed are per student.

- **Letter to the Family**
- **Student Activity Sheets 1–5**

Teacher Resources

No resources required.

Student Materials

Quantities listed are per pair of students, unless otherwise noted.

- **calculator (one per student)**
- **centimeter ruler**
- **colored pencils, one box**
- **brochures on savings plans from a local bank**

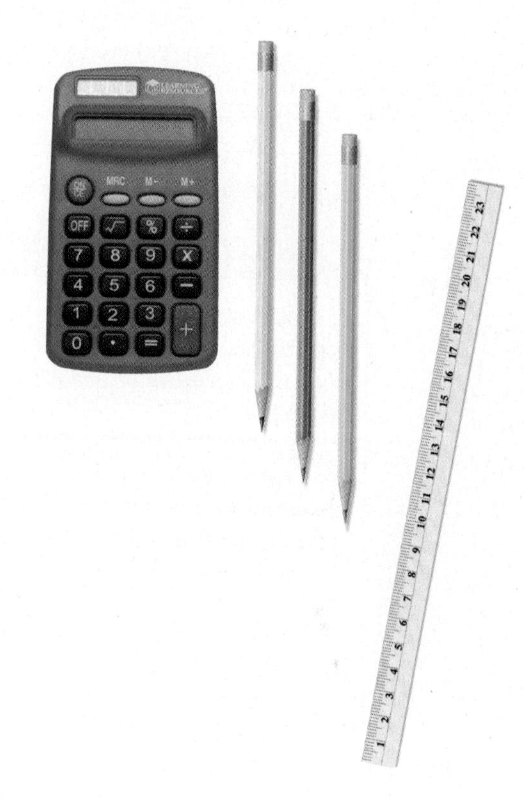

BRITANNICA

Mathematics in Context

Student Material and Teaching Notes

Contents

1.00 KG

1.92

Veggies-R-Us
Tomatoes
packed on: 05.27.05
sell by:
$/kg 3.20
Net weight 1.250 kg
PRICE
$4.00
0221311 465683

Sale Price

Dear Student,

This unit is about the ways in which fractions, decimals, and percents are related.

Do you purchase items that need to be weighed? How is the final price determined? Calculating per unit prices and total prices requires multiplication with fraction and decimal numbers.

Do you buy your favorite items on sale? Next time you shop, notice the sale discount. Sale discounts are usually expressed in percents.

In this unit, you will use fractions and percents to find sale prices. You can use models like a double number line, a percent bar, or a ratio table to help you make calculations.

You will investigate the percent by which a photograph increases or decreases in size when you enlarge or reduce it on a photocopier.

You will also use fractions and percents to describe survey results.

While working on this unit, look for ads that list discounts in percents and newspaper articles that give survey results. Share what you find with the class.

All the situations in this unit will help you perfect your operations with fractions, decimals, and percents. Good luck.

Sincerely,

The Mathematics in Context Development Team

Section Focus

This section uses students' prior knowledge and experiences to solve problems that involve finding the cost of produce that is sold by weight. Three estimation strategies are introduced to estimate the cost of produce: rounding, changing decimals to fractions and multiplying, and using a double number line. At the end of the section, students use these strategies to find the exact answers. They also use number sense to determine the correct placement of the decimal point in the product of two decimal numbers. The instructional focus of Section A is to:

- **multiply decimals and fractions using a double number line and**
- **identify the appropriate placement of the decimal point in decimal multiplication.**

Pacing and Planning

Day 1: Scales		Student pages 1–4
INTRODUCTION	Problems 1–3	Discuss the pricing and weight of produce.
CLASSWORK	Problems 4–8	Read a produce scale and calculate the cost of Red Delicious apples.
HOMEWORK	Problems 9–11	Calculate the cost of different types of apples.

Day 2: Veggies-R-Us		Student pages 5–7
INTRODUCTION	Problem 12	Identify correct prices for produce.
CLASSWORK	Problems 13–16	Explore decimal calculations by calculating the cost of different weights of apples.
HOMEWORK	Problems 17–19	Identify appropriate placement of the decimal point when calculating the cost of produce.

Day 3: Summary		Student pages 7–10
INTRODUCTION	Review homework.	Review homework from Day 2.
CLASSWORK	Check Your Work and For Further Reflection	Students self-assess their estimation and computation methods.
HOMEWORK	Additional Practice, Section A, page 35	More practice computing with decimals and fractions.

Additional Resources: *Number Tools*, pages 16–21, 25, 34, and 111–113

Materials

Student Resources

Quantities listed are per student.

- Letter to the Family

Teachers Resources

No resources required.

Student Materials

Quantities listed are per student.

- Calculator

* See Hints and Comments for optional materials.

Learning Lines

Concepts *Number Sense* and *Strategies*

Three multiplication estimation strategies are introduced in this section. The first estimation strategy, rounding numbers to find quick estimates, builds on students' number sense. The second estimation strategy involves converting decimals to fractions. Many decimals are easily converted to fractions, which some students may find easier to use. For example, instead of multiplying 0.25 times $1.80, students may find it easier to multiply $\frac{1}{4}$ times 1.80, or take $\frac{1}{4}$ of 1.80. Students can use number sense; "take $\frac{1}{4}$ of" is the same as "take half" (0.90) and then "take half again" (0.45). Or students can calculate $\frac{1}{4}$ of 1 (0.25) and $\frac{1}{4}$ of 0.80 (0.20) and add to get a total of 0.45.

The third estimation strategy involves using a double number line, which helps students to visualize the relationship between the price of the apples and the amount purchased. If, for example, 1 kg of apples cost $2.40, students can estimate a cost at or near 1.75 kg by first doubling $2.40 to determine what 2 kg will cost. Then, students repeatedly find the number halfway between two numbers:

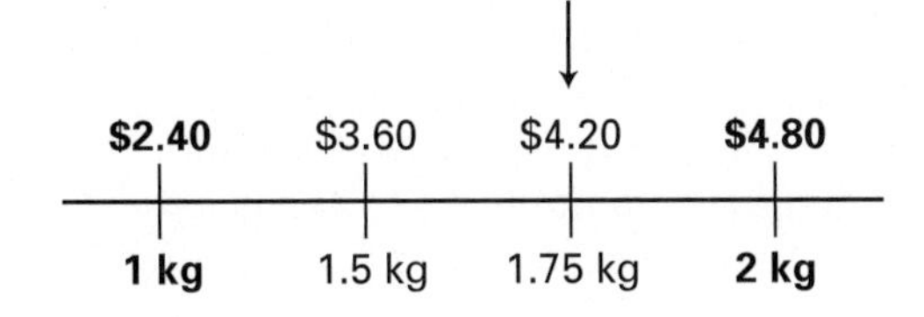

Models

In this section the *double number line* from the unit *Models You Can Count On* is revisited in the context of a supermarket produce department. Students use the scale and the price per kilogram to estimate and calculate the cost of produce. Like the ratio table, the double number line generates equivalent ratios, but the order of the numbers is maintained, and in this way gives the students visual support.

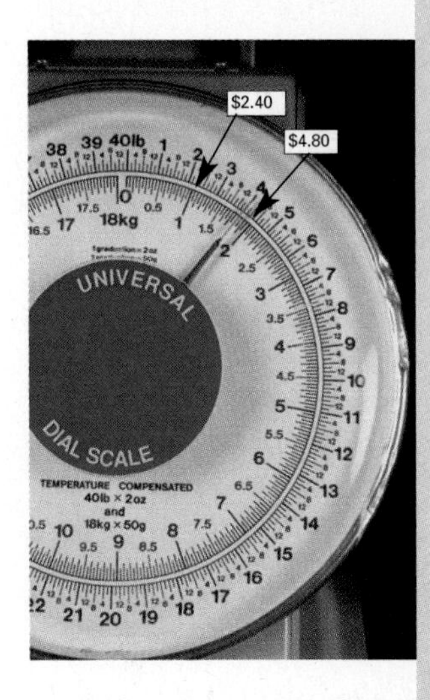

At the End of this Section: Learning Outcomes

Students are able to use estimation strategies to multiply fractions and decimals and also find exact answers. They can use number sense to multiply two decimal numbers.

Produce Pricing

Notes

To introduce this section you can have a whole class discussion about students' experiences with buying fruits and vegetables.

Or you might want to start this section with a class discussion about the use of scales for weighing products and the common measurement units used to weigh them. Ask, *What measurement units have you seen on scales in the grocery store?* (ounces, pounds, grams, kilograms)

Ask students to name objects that weigh about 1 kg.

Produce Pricing

Scales

Save Supermarket displays fresh fruits and vegetables so customers can select individual pieces and put what they want into bags. When customers check out, cashiers weigh the produce and enter a produce code that calculates the prices.

Many customers want to know the cost of their selections before they check out. Ms. Vander, the produce manager, put a dial scale near the fruit-and-vegetable counter so customers can weigh their own produce. Customers can use the price per weight to **estimate** the costs.

Reaching All Learners

Vocabulary Building

Be sure students understand what is meant by *estimate*. Some students may be tempted to think of an estimate as a rounded answer rather than the result of a calculation that uses close, but not exact numbers. Students should realize that an estimate should be easy to calculate.

Accommodation

If students have not yet developed points of reference for the weight of 1 kg, you may tell them that a kilogram is equal to 2.2 lb. You might show them 1 kg of any fruit or vegetable.

Hints and Comments

Materials

fruits or vegetables (optional, one kilogram per class)

Overview

This page introduces the context of the section: weighing fruits or vegetables at a supermarket to estimate the cost of each variety based on its price per kilogram. There are no problems on this page.

About the Mathematics

Some students may have learned in science that kilograms refer to mass, while pounds refer to weight. Conventionally, however, countries that use the metric system use kilograms as a measure of weight.

Students may remember that metric measurement is based on the decimal system. Each metric unit is one-tenth the value of the next largest unit. To give students another point of reference, you may mention that one gram is one one-thousandth (one-tenth of one-tenth of one-tenth) of a kilogram and a paper clip weighs about 1 g.

Produce Pricing

Notes

1 The price of the apples was chosen to be a number that was easy to work with. Students should be able to find the price by finding half of $2.40 and then adding that to $2.40.

2 Be sure that all students are able to read the dial scale. The point is for students to realize that this is more than $1\frac{1}{2}$.

3 Students should be encouraged to estimate; the goal at this point is **not** to calculate the exact price.

After students complete these problems, be sure to discuss students' strategies.

Carol is a customer at Save Supermarket. She wants to buy $1\frac{1}{2}$ kilograms (kg) of Red Delicious apples.

1. What is the cost of $1\frac{1}{2}$ kg of apples if they are priced at $2.40 per kilogram?

Carol places some apples on the scale. A picture of the scale is shown here.

2. Does Carol have the amount of apples she wants? Explain.

Carol decides to buy all of the apples on the scale. She wonders what this will cost.

3. Estimate the total cost of Carol's apple selection. How did you arrive at your estimate?

Reaching All Learners

Intervention

Students struggling with problem 1 could be asked to find the price of $1\frac{1}{2}$ kg of apples if they cost $2.00 a kg.

English Language Learners

Students may not be familiar with the fruits used in this section. You can provide samples and may want to change the fruits to ones that are more familiar. However, the prices should not change because the numbers have been carefully selected.

Solutions and Samples

1. One and one-half kilograms of apples will cost $3.60. Strategies will vary.

   Sample strategies:

   Strategy 1

   One-half kilogram of apples costs half of $2.40, or $1.20. So $1\frac{1}{2}$ kg of apples costs

   $2.40 + $1.20 = $3.60.

   Strategy 2

   Two kilograms of apples cost $4.80. The price for $1\frac{1}{2}$ kg of apples is halfway between $2.40 and $4.80, which is $3.60.

2. Answers will vary. Sample student responses:

   No. The scale shows that the apples weigh 1.8 kg, which is too much if Carol wants to buy exactly $1\frac{1}{2}$ kg of apples.

   Yes. The scale shows a weight between 1.5 and 2 kg, which is close.

3. Estimates will vary. Sample student responses:

   The apples on the scale weigh 1.8 kg, which is about 2 kg of apples. Apples cost $2.40 for 1 kg, so 2 kg cost $4.80. So the cost of 1.8 kg is a little less than $4.80.

   Using the answer from Problem 1, I can find that the price of 1.75 kg is $4.20.

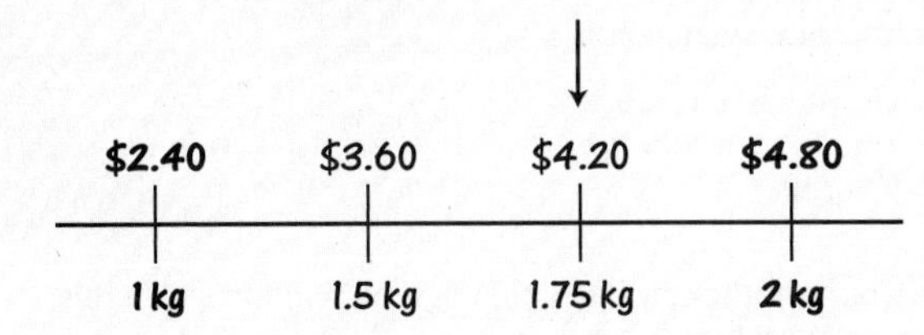

   This means that my estimate should be between $4.20 and $4.80, but closer to $4.20 because 1.8 is closer to 1.75 than it is to 2.0 kg.

Hints and Comments

Materials

transparency of the scale on Student Book page 2 (optional, one per class)

Overview

Students estimate and compute the cost of a certain weight of apples.

About the Mathematics

In the unit *Fraction Times*, students developed four different strategies for multiplying whole numbers with decimals within the context of money. Each method is illustrated below using the example 4 × $2.49.

- repeated addition

  $2.49 + $2.49 + $2.49 + $2.49 = $9.96

- number sense

  4 × $2.50 = $10.00, and $2.49 is $0.01 away from $2.50, so 4 × $2.49 = $10.00 – $0.04 = $9.96

- the distributive property

  $2.49 can be split up into $2.00 + $0.40 + $0.09, so 4 × $2.49 = 4 × $2.00 + 4 × $0.40 + 4 × $0.09 = $9.96)

- a ratio table:

Weight (in kg)	1	2	4
Cost (in dollars)	2.49	4.98	9.96

Students use these strategies, their estimation skills, and their ability to convert between decimals and fractions as they find the product of two decimals.

Comments About the Solutions

1. Allow students to develop and use their own strategy. Suggest that students make a note of the way they arrived at their answer.
2. If students are having difficulty reading the scale, suggest that they estimate the weight between the two whole numbers (1 kg and 2 kg) and then ask for a more precise estimate (between $1\frac{1}{2}$ and 2 kg, almost 2 kg, a little more than $1\frac{1}{2}$ kg, $1\frac{3}{4}$ kg, or 1.8 kg).
3. If students are having difficulty estimating, have them use a transparency of the picture of the scale to write the prices of 1 kg and 2 kg next to the marks on the scale. This may help them to visualize the price that the pointer of the scale indicates.

Produce Pricing

Notes

This page gives students an opportunity to explore a variety of strategies for finding the price.

4c Students may need to review a double number line. One possibility is to draw a double number line that all students can see and start by filling in the prices corresponding to whole numbers.

5 Students may use the ratio table to estimate or to find an exact answer by using tenths.

Carol's friends Pablo, Lia, and Pam are helping Carol estimate the cost of her apples. They are waiting to use the scale after Carol is finished. To help Carol, they make several suggestions to estimate the cost.

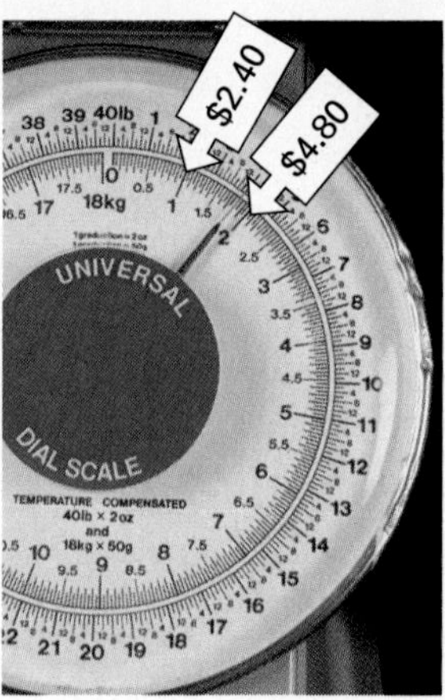

Pablo says, "That's almost 2 kilograms of apples."

Lia states, "That's about $1\frac{3}{4}$ kilograms of apples."

Pam suggests, "Use the scale as a double number line."

4. a. How will Pablo find the answer? What will Pablo estimate?

b. How will Lia calculate the answer? What will she estimate?

c. How will Pam use a double number line to estimate the cost of the apples?

You may remember another strategy that can be used to solve this problem: using a **ratio table**.

5. Show how you would use a ratio table to estimate the cost of the apples.

Reaching All Learners

Visual Learners

This is a good place to help students think back to their previous work with double number lines. In this case, the line is slightly curved and more vertical than double number lines that students may be more familiar with.

Advanced Learners

You can ask students what the difference is between the double number line solution and the ratio table solution. For some students, the differences may be only the order in which the numbers appear, while for others, the strategies may be quite different. Some students may be able to see the double number line as an ordered ratio table.

Solutions and Samples

4. a. Pablo's strategy: If 1 kg of apples costs $2.40, then 2 kg cost twice that amount, or $4.80. Since the apples weigh less than 2 kg, the cost would be less than $4.80. So Pablo's estimate is just under $4.80.

b. Lia's strategy:

Since 1 kg of apples costs $2.40,

$\frac{1}{2}$ kg costs $1.20, and $\frac{1}{4}$ kg costs $0.60.

Then $\frac{3}{4}$ kg costs $1.20 + $ 0.60 = $1.80.

So $1\frac{3}{4}$ kg cost $2.40 + $1.80 = $4.20, and her estimate should be a little more than $4.20.

c. Pam's strategy:

On a double number line, the weight of 1.5 kg is halfway between 1 kg and 2 kg, and $3.60 is halfway between $2.40 and $4.80.

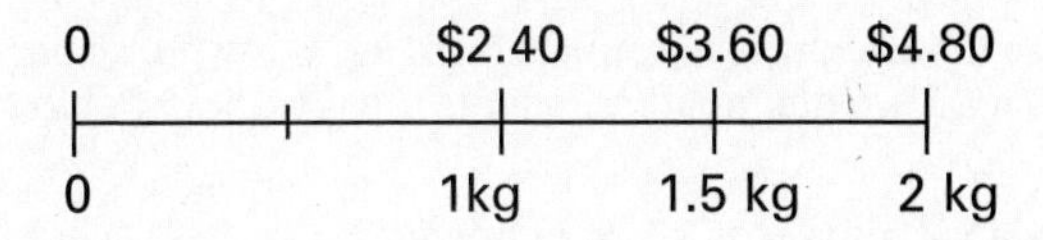

The weight of 1.75 kg is halfway between 1.5 kg and 2 kg, and $4.20 is halfway between $3.60 and $4.80.

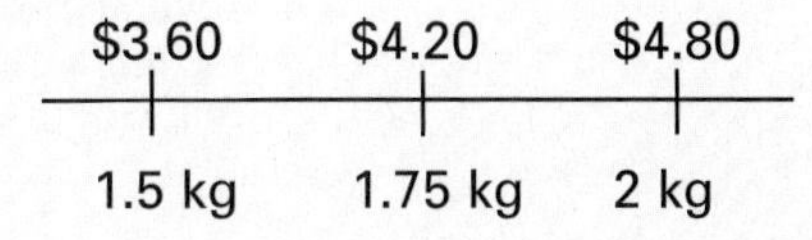

The pointer is pointing to a number a little above 1.75. So Pam's estimate is a little more than $4.20.

5. Answers will vary. Some students may notice that ratio tables are similar to double number lines. The difference with the double number line is that the paired numbers (ratios) need to be ordered.

Hints and Comments

Overview

Students read about three strategies to estimate the cost of a certain weight of apples and explain how each estimation strategy can be used.

About the Mathematics

On this page, three estimation strategies are suggested:

- rounding numbers to make them easier to compute with;
- changing decimals to fractions; and
- using a double number line to visualize the relationship between the price and the weight.

The relationships between the weights on the scale and the corresponding prices can be illustrated using a double number line as shown below.

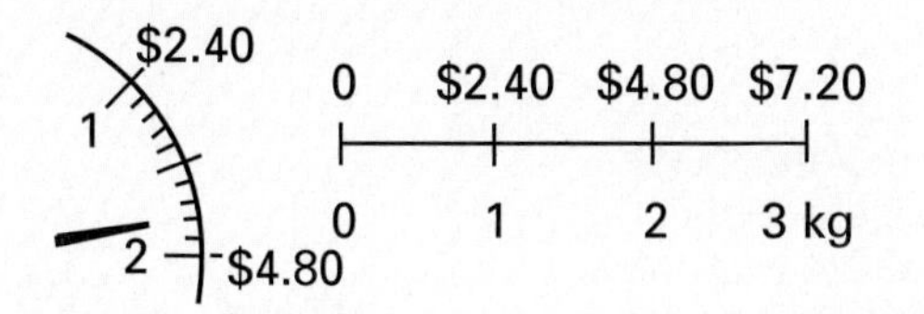

Planning

Discuss students' answers and explanations. Compare how their different strategies affect the estimates. Discuss what accounts for "good" estimates, and help students understand that each strategy can give an appropriate estimate. Stress the importance of students understanding all three strategies. Also stress how the context of a situation determines how precise an answer must be.

Comments About the Solutions

4. Students read a produce scale, find an estimate using three different methods, and explain how each method works. It is important that students' explanations are mathematically sound.

c. To find the price of $1\frac{3}{4}$ kg, students may implicitly use the distributive property. Others may reason that $\frac{3}{4} = \frac{1}{2} + \frac{1}{4}$ and compute the price of $\frac{1}{2}$ kg and halve it to get the price of $\frac{1}{4}$ kg. Still other students may reason that $1\frac{3}{4}$ kg is the price of 2 kg minus the price of $\frac{1}{4}$ kg.

Produce Pricing

Notes

All of these problems ask for estimations. Students should be encouraged to use whole numbers and benchmark fractions to make their estimates.

8 To save time, provide either pre-drawn circles or copies of the scale face.

9 When making their estimates, students should realize that they may use $2.90 or even $3.00 rather than $2.89.

9 You may need to refer students back to the scale on the previous page to find the weight of Carol's apples (about 1.8 kg).

10 and 11 The double number line or the ratio table is particularly useful for solving these problems.

When Carol is finished with the scale, Pam weighs 10 apples she selected. This scale shows the weight of Pam's apples.

6. Estimate what Pam will pay for her apples.

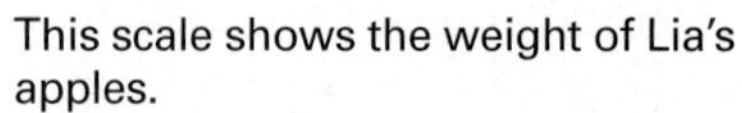

This scale shows the weight of Lia's apples.

7. Estimate what Lia will pay for her apples.

Pablo places his apples on the scale.

8. **a.** Suppose the weight of his apples is 2.1 kg. Copy the scale's dial and draw the pointer so it represents the weight of Pablo's apples.

b. What will Pablo pay for 2.1 kg of apples?

Save Supermarket sells several kinds of apples, including Red Delicious and Granny Smith.

Suppose Carol, Pablo, and Pam bought the same weight of Granny Smith apples instead of Red Delicious apples.

9. Using the scale weights from problems 6–8, estimate the price each person will pay for the same weight of Granny Smith apples.

10. Pam wants to buy additional apples. She has $8. Estimate the total weight of Red Delicious apples Pam can buy.

11. Pablo has $2.50 to spend on Granny Smith apples. Estimate the total weight of apples Pablo can buy.

Assessment Pyramid

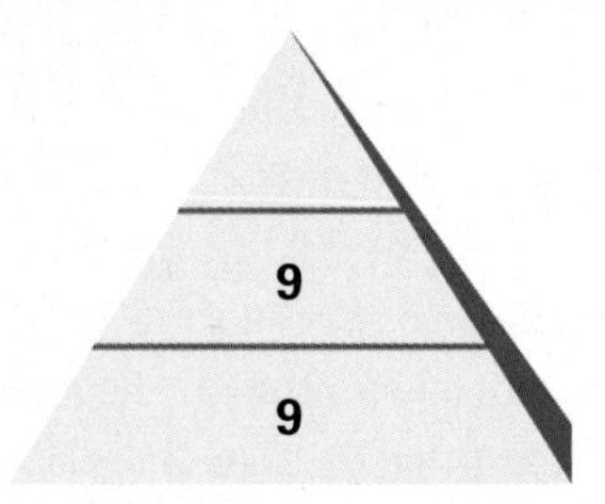

Use estimation strategies.

Develop number sense.

Reaching All Learners

Accommodation

Some students may need a large copy of the scale for problem 8. Students with small motor problems could be asked to use a toothpick or another small stick to show what the scale would look like.

Intervention

For problem 10, it may be helpful for some students to make a table of the prices and weights that they have already found so that they know where to start making their estimates

Solutions and Samples

6. Estimates will vary. Accept estimates in the range of \$6.00–\$7.20. Strategies will vary. Sample strategies:

Strategy 1

Pam is buying a little more than $2\frac{1}{2}$ kg of apples. One kilogram of apples costs \$2.40, 2 kg costs \$4.80, and $\frac{1}{2}$ kg costs \$1.20. So, $2\frac{1}{2}$ kg of apples costs \$4.80 + \$1.20 = \$6.00. Pam has to pay a little more than \$6.00.

Strategy 2

Pam is buying about 1 kg more than Carol. If Carol is spending between \$3.60 and \$4.80, then Pam will spend \$2.40 more than that, or between \$6.00 and \$7.20, but closer to \$6.00.

7. Estimates will vary. Accept estimates in the range of \$1.20 – \$2.40. Strategies will vary. Sample strategies:

Strategy 1

Lia buys 1 kg less than Carol, so she pays \$2.40 less than Carol or between \$1.20 and \$2.40.

Strategy 2

Lia is buying about $\frac{3}{4}$ kg of apples. This is $\frac{1}{2}$ kg (\$1.20) plus $\frac{1}{4}$ kg (\$0.60). So she will pay about \$1.80.

Strategy 3, Using a double number line:

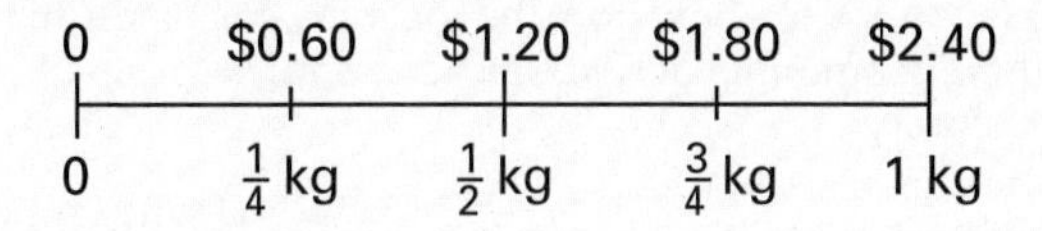

8. a.

b. Pablo is buying 2.1 kg of apples.
One kilogram costs \$2.40, so 2 kg costs \$4.80.
0.1 kg is one tenth of 1 kg, so
0.1 kg costs one tenth of \$2.40, which is \$0.24.
2.1 kg cost \$4.80 + \$0.24 = \$5.04.

9. Answers and strategies will vary. Sample responses:

- Carol's purchase, 1.8 kg
  1 kg costs \$2.89 or about \$2.90.
  0.1 or $\frac{1}{10}$ of a kg costs about \$0.29
  0.8 kg is 8 times as much, and 8 × \$0.29 is about 8 × \$0.30 = \$2.40. So Carol's apples cost about \$2.90 + \$2.40 = \$5.30.
- Pam's purchase, a little more than 2.5 kg;
  2.5 kg is half of half of 10 kg:

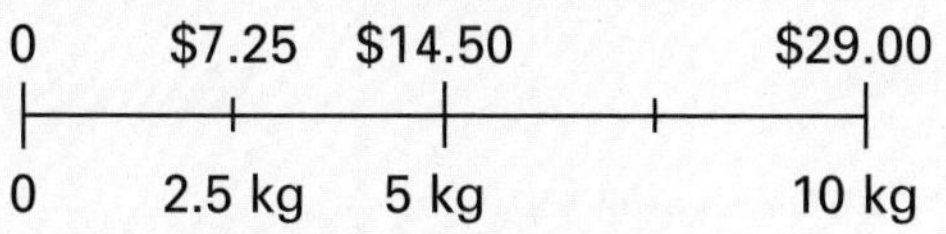

  So Pam's apples cost about \$7.25.
  Or: Pam's purchase, 2.6 kg
  2 kg costs about 2 × \$2.90 = 5.80.
  0.1 or 1/10 of a kg costs about \$0.29.
  0.6 kg costs about 6 × \$0.30 = \$1.80.
  So Pam's apples cost about \$5.80 + \$1.80 = \$7.60.
- Lia's purchase: Lia buys 1 kg of apples less than Carol, who estimates paying about \$5.30.
  So Lia's apples cost about \$5.30 – \$2.90.
  \$5.30 – \$3.00 = \$2.30, so \$5.30 – \$2.90 = \$2.40.
- Pablo's purchase: Pablo is buying 2.1 kg of apples.
  One kilogram costs about \$2.90.
  2 kg costs about \$5.80.
  0.1 kg costs one-tenth of \$2.90, that is \$0.29.
  2.1 kg cost about \$5.80 + \$0.29 = \$6.09.

10. Pam could buy $3\frac{1}{3}$ kg of Red Delicious.

Sample strategies:

Strategy 1

Since 1 kg of Red Delicious apples costs \$2.40, 3 kg cost \$7.20. She has \$0.80 left. This \$0.80 is one-third of \$2.40, so she could buy $\frac{1}{3}$ kg more apples, or $3\frac{1}{3}$ kg of apples all together.

Strategy 2, using a ratio table:

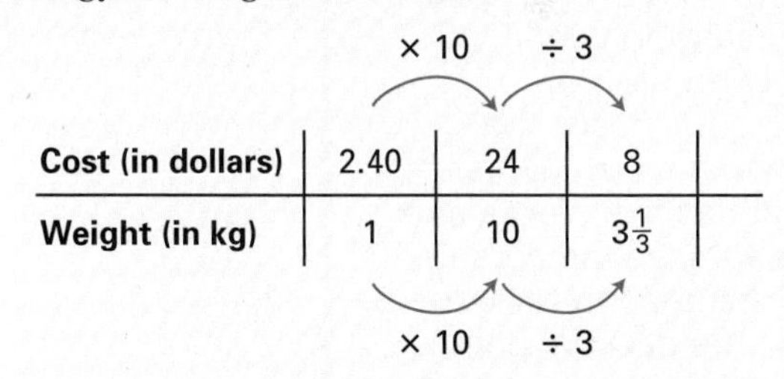

Cost (in dollars)	2.40	24	8	
Weight (in kg)	1	10	$3\frac{1}{3}$	

11. Answers will vary. Sample student responses:

Pablo doesn't have enough money for 1 kg (\$2.89).
$\frac{1}{2}$ kg costs about \$1.45 (\$2.50 – \$1.45 = \$1.05 left).
$\frac{1}{4}$ kg costs about \$0.73 (\$1.05 – \$0.73 = \$0.32 left).
$\frac{1}{8}$ kg costs about 0.37
So he can buy $\frac{1}{2} + \frac{1}{4} + \frac{1}{8}$ kg, or just under $\frac{7}{8}$ kg of Granny Smith apples.
Granny Smith apples cost about \$2.90 per kilogram.
0.1 kg costs about \$0.29.
\$2.90 – \$0.30 = \$2.60 is the cost for 0.9 kg of Granny Smith apples, so he can buy a little less than 0.9 kg.

See Hints and Comments on page 60.

A Produce Pricing

Notes

Up to this point, students have used their fraction skills to find prices. Here the focus shifts to introducing multiplication of decimals.

13 The goal of this problem is to formalize the fact that the operation in this case is multiplication. Some students may need to think through what they have been doing in order to realize that they, in fact, have been multiplying.

14 Notice that these problems are in groups, each starting with a whole number of kilograms. Resist the urge to have students count decimal places and instead have them use their estimation skills to place the decimal point.

Veggies-R-Us

Some supermarkets require customers to use special machines to print the cost of produce before they check out. At Veggies-R-Us, customers place items on the scale, they key in the type of produce, and the machine prints the cost. A sticker for a tomato purchase is shown on the left.

There is something wrong with the machine! Sometimes it gives incorrect prices. The produce manager is checking the receipts to get a sense of how many are wrong.

12. Use estimation to determine which receipts are wrong. Decide whether the machine is overcharging or undercharging customers.

The storeowner repaired the machine so that it functions properly.

13. Use **arrow language** to show how the machine calculates the costs of different amounts of Red Delicious apples priced at $2.40 per kilogram.

14. Without using a calculator, describe how to calculate the cost of these amounts of apples at $2.40 per kilogram.

a. 15 kg
b. 1.5 kg
c. 4 kg
d. 0.4 kg
e. 0.04 kg
f. 7 kg
g. 0.7 kg

Assessment Pyramid

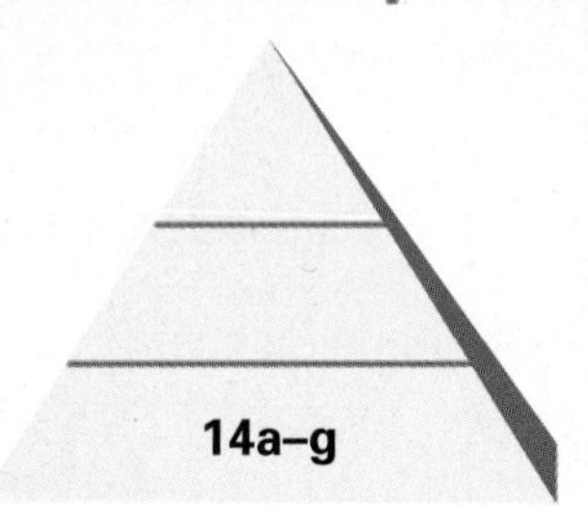

Use number sense to multiply two decimal numbers.

Reaching All Learners

English Language Learners

Ask students if they have ever shopped in a place where they used a scale like this. Some may have seen one in the bulk foods section of a grocery store, or they may have seen a store employee using one in the deli department.

Intervention

Some students may need help reading the labels and discovering what information they need. It may be useful to give them a copy of the labels that they can use to circle or highlight the relevant information.

Solutions and Samples

12. The store is overcharging customers for Red Delicious apples. The store is undercharging customers for peaches.

Explanations will vary. Sample explanations:

- Red Delicious Apples sticker: The weight is between 1 and 2 kg. The apples cost $2.40 for 1 kg, and $4.80 for 2 kg, so $31.92 for 1.330 kg is far too high.
- Peaches sticker: The weight is $2\frac{1}{2}$ kg. The peaches cost $0.66 for 1 kg and $1.32 for 2 kg. One-half of a kilogram costs $0.33, so the customer has to pay $1.32 + $0.33 = $1.65. The sticker price is far too low.
- Grapes sticker: Grapes cost $2.85 for 1 kg and the customer bought $\frac{1}{4}$ kg less than 1 kg. $\frac{1}{4}$ of $2.85 is about $0.70, so the customer should pay about $2.85 − $0.70 = $2.15. The sticker price is reasonable.

13. *Weight of apples* $\xrightarrow{\times 2.4}$ *Cost of apples*

14. a. The price is $36.00.

Sample strategy: 15 = 10 + 5.

So 10 × $2.40 + 5 × $2.40 = $24.00 + $12.00 = $36.00.

b. The price is $3.60. Sample strategy: It is one-tenth of the weight in **a**, so it will cost one-tenth of the price in **a**.

c. The price is $9.60. Sample strategy using a ratio table:

Weight (in kg)	1	2	4
Cost (in dollars)	2.40	4.80	9.60

d. The price is $0.96. Sample strategy: It is one-tenth of the weight in **c**, so it will cost one tenth of the price in **c**.

e. The price is $0.10 ($0.096 rounded). Sample strategy: It is one-tenth of the weight in **d**, so it will cost one tenth of the price in **d**.

f. The price is $16.80. Sample strategy:

The amount 7 kg can be thought of as 4 kg + 3 kg. Using answers from problem **c** and problem **b** (3 kg is double 1.5 kg), the price for 7 kg is $9.60 + 2 × $3.60 = $9.60 + $7.20 = $16.80.

g. The price is $1.68. Sample strategy: It is one-tenth of the weight in **f**, so it will cost one tenth of the price in **f**.

Hints and Comments

Overview

Students estimate to determine the accuracy of the total prices on different produce stickers that show unit prices, weights, and total prices. Students describe how to calculate prices for different weights of apples without using a calculator.

About the Mathematics

These problems invite students to round numbers or to use fractions to make estimation strategies easier to use. The use of these strategies allows students to use number sense. These problems can be solved to different degrees of accuracy using various estimating strategies.

- The weight can be estimated between two whole number weight measures. See for example the strategy shown for the Red Delicious apples sticker.
- The cost can be estimated using the unit cost. See, for example, the strategy shown for the Grapes sticker.

In problem 13, arrow language reinforces that multiplication is the operation used to calculate the cost. This method resembles how the machine calculates prices by multiplying the weight times the price per unit (kilogram). Arrow language is introduced in the algebra unit *Expressions and Formulas*.

Planning

You may want to use the Extension to help students focus on the placement of the decimal point in the product, which foreshadows the problems on Student Book page 8.

Comments About the Solutions

12. Encourage students to explain how they found their answers. Because of the outrageously incorrect prices, rough estimates are sufficient to see which price stickers are wrong.

14. The solutions provided include several strategies. Traditional algorithms are not necessary. Eventually, students will know a variety of ways to multiply decimals. Observe whether students use the relationships between the weights in problem **14** to calculate the prices. (For example, the answer for **14b** is related to that of **14a**, the answer for **14e** is related to that of **14d**, **14f** can rely on **14c** and **14b**.)

Extension

Ask students to describe the mistakes made by the weighing machine in each case. (Sample response: The digits in the answer are correct, but the decimal point is in the wrong place.)

A Produce Pricing

Notes

This page introduces the use of the calculator to solve decimal multiplication problems.

15 You can use this problem to find out students' understandings or misunderstandings about multiplying by a number smaller than one.

16 Students may have difficulty determining a second way. Encourage them to use what they know about the meaning of ×.

Paul calculated the price for 0.8 kg of Red Delicious apples at Save Supermarket. He used his calculator and made these entries.

0.8 [×] $2.40 [=]

His calculator displayed 1.92 as the total.

Mary disagrees.

15. **Reflect** Is Mary right, or is Paul's calculator correct? Defend your position.

16. Describe two ways to use a calculator to determine the cost of $\frac{3}{4}$ kg of walnuts priced at $7.98 per kilogram.

Broken Calculator

Ms. Vander of Save Supermarket likes the calculating scale that customers use at Veggies-R-Us. She decides to keep a calculator next to her dial scale. Customers can calculate the exact cost of their produce before they check out.

Unfortunately, the calculator has been used so much that the **decimal point** key no longer works.

Assessment Pyramid

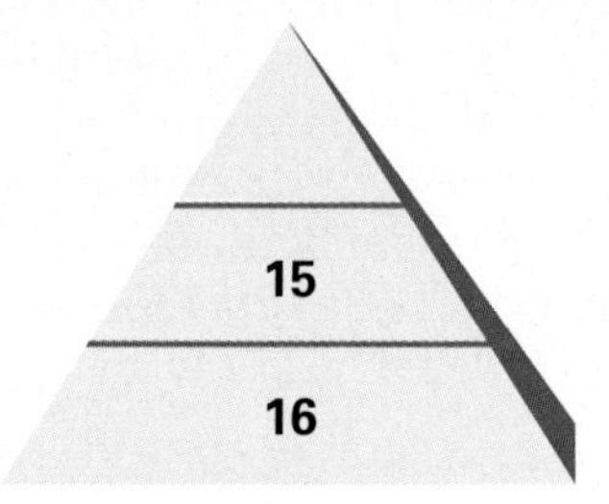

Develop number sense.

Use estimation strategies.

Reaching All Learners

Intervention

If students are having difficulty understanding problem 16, begin by asking about the cost of $\frac{3}{4}$ kg. Most students can easily see that this would be less than the price of a whole kilogram.

Extension

Have students describe two ways to estimate the cost of $\frac{3}{4}$ kg of walnuts priced at $7.98 when you do not have a calculator.

Solutions and Samples

15. The answer given by the calculator is correct. The cost of less than 1 kg of apples is less than $2.40.

16. Answers will vary. Sample student responses:

Key in [3] [÷] [4] [×] [7] [.] [9] [8]
Key in [7] [.] [9] [8] [×] [3] [÷] [4]
Key in [.] [7] [5] [×] [7] [.] [9] [8]

Reaching All Learners (Extension)

Sample responses:

- You can use a ratio table.
  $7.98 is about $8.00.

Weight (kg)	1	$\frac{1}{2}$	$\frac{1}{4}$	$\frac{3}{4}$
Cost	$8	$4	$2	$6

- $\frac{1}{4}$ of $8 is $2 and $\frac{3}{4}$ is three times as much, so the cost is 3 × $2 = $6.
- You can use a double number line to make these computations.

Hints and Comments

Materials

calculators (one per student)

Overview

Students describe two ways of using a calculator to determine the cost of a fraction of 1 kg of apples.

About the Mathematics

The context in problem 16 should help students to understand that multiplication doesn't always result in an answer greater than the factors being multiplied. This concept will be revisited in the unit *Reflections on Number*. In *Fraction Times*, the context of money is used to reinforce the relationships between fractions and decimals.

Planning

You might have a class discussion to emphasize that a calculation involving multiplication was used to solve each problem and that multiplication does not always produce an answer greater than either factor.

Comments About the Solutions

16. Students may want to change the fraction $\frac{3}{4}$ into a decimal first. They may think of this fraction in terms of money and realize that three quarters is the same as $0.75. Thus, $\frac{3}{4}$ is 0.75.

Produce Pricing

Notes

Make sure that students understand that they cannot enter a decimal point into the calculator.

17 The three parts of this problem show students how they can use estimation and multiplication of whole numbers to determine the product of two decimal numbers.

18 Encourage students to use estimation and number sense as shown in the Solutions and Samples column rather than the counting decimal places and placing the decimal point accordingly.

19 Remind students to use estimation to determine where the decimal point should be placed.

Sean weighs 2.63 kg of strawberries priced at $4.32 per kilogram. He thinks he can use the calculator in spite of the defective decimal point key.

17. a. Make a low estimate and a high estimate of the cost of Sean's strawberries.

b. Describe how Sean will use the calculator to find the exact cost of his strawberries.

c. Find the cost of Sean's strawberries.

18. Use your answer to part **c** of problem 17 to determine the prices of these amounts:

a. 0.263 kg of strawberries

b. 26.3 kg of strawberries

19. The calculator is still broken. Use the information below to find the actual cost of each strawberry purchase. Describe how you found each answer.

Customer	Weight	Calculator Display
Sally	3.98 kg	171936
Devin	1.72 kg	74304
Niya	0.39 kg	16848

Assessment Pyramid

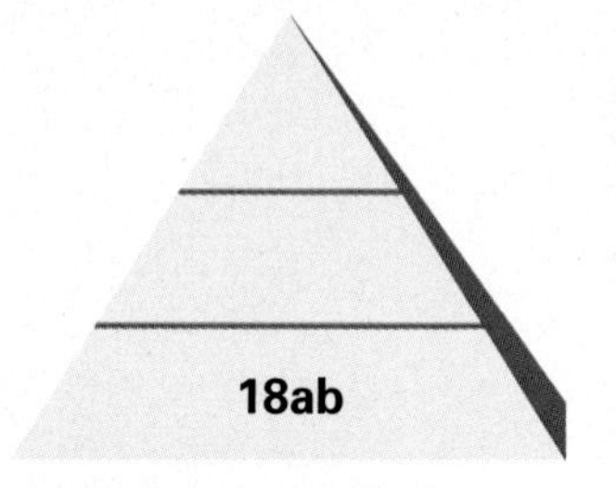

Use number sense to multiply two decimal numbers.

Reaching All Learners

Extension

Ask students to relate the answers to problems 17c and 18 to what they know about multiplying and dividing by ten.

Solutions and Samples

17. a. Answers will vary. A possible answer: A low estimate would be 2 times $4 or $8. A high estimate would be 3 times $4 or $12.

b. Sean will multiply 263 by 432 on his calculator.

c. The cost of the strawberries is $11.36. Using the broken calculator to multiply 263 × 432 (the unit price and weight without decimal points), Sean got 113,616. Since the price should be between $8 and $12, the decimal point should be placed between the 1 and the 3, and the price rounded to the nearest cent.

18. a. The price is $1.14.

Since 0.263 is $\frac{1}{10}$ of 2.63, the price must be $\frac{1}{10}$ of $11.36, which is $1.136 or $1.14.

b. The price is $113.60.

Since 26.3 is ten times 2.63, the price must be ten times $11.36, which is $113.60.

19. Strategies will vary.

- Sally's strawberries cost $17.19. Sample student response:

  The weight is almost 4 kg, and the cost is about $4/kg. Four times $4 is equal to $16.00. The cost should be about $16.00, so place the decimal point between the 7 and 1 (17.1936), and round to the nearest cent.

- Devon's strawberries cost $7.43. Sample student response:

  The weight is almost 2 kg, and the cost is about $4/kg. Two times $4 equals $8. The cost should be under $8. Place the decimal point between the 7 and the 4 (7.4304) and round to the nearest cent.

- Niya's stawberries cost $1.68. Sample student response:

  The weight is a little more than $\frac{1}{3}$ kg. The price is a little less than $4.50/kg. One-third of $4.50 is $1.50. The estimated price should be a little more than $1.50, so place the decimal point between the 1 and the 6 and round to $1.68.

Hints and Comments

Overview

Students estimate prices to find the correct placement of decimal points in a calculator display that is broken.

About the Mathematics

Since our number system is based on units of ten, students, when given the opportunity, are easily able to compute successive products and quotients involving powers of ten. (See note for problem 18 below.)

Planning

Students may work on problems 17–19 in pairs or small groups. Problem 19 may be assigned for homework. Discuss students' answers and strategies for problems 17 and 18 before they continue with problem 19.

Comments About the Solutions

17. Encourage students to use number sense. You may need to discuss why answers should be rounded to the nearest cent.

18. Have students compare their answers for problems 17c, 18a, and 18b. You might give students an opportunity to find 10 times or $\frac{1}{10}$ of a decimal number. You might look at *Number Tools,* for additional problems. You might even have students use their calculators to solve the following problems:

$\frac{1}{10}$ of $37.65   100 times $37.65

10 times $37.65 $\frac{1}{100}$ of $37.65

Then after a class discussion, have them do the following without their calculators:

$\frac{1}{10}$ of $2.97 $\frac{1}{100}$ of $2.97

10 times $2.97 $\frac{1}{1000}$ of $2,367.98

100 times $2.97

19. Note that the cost of Niya's strawberries could be solved using the cost of Sally's strawberries, since the difference between the weights involves the placement of the decimal point. Because students know from Sally's data that 3.98 kg of strawberries cost $17.19, they could estimate that 0.39 kg will cost a bit less than one-tenth of that, or about $1.72.

Produce Pricing

Notes

The Summary for this section reiterates each of the strategies used in the section. Be sure to go through the Summary carefully, perhaps having students read parts aloud. It is critical that students understand each of the strategies.

Produce Pricing

Summary

There are many ways to **estimate** or find the cost of produce.

You may use number tools such as a double number line, a ratio table, or a calculator.

For example, there are several strategies to find the cost of 1.8 kg of Golden Delicious apples priced at $1.60 per kilogram.

- Estimate by rounding **decimals** to whole numbers.

You might reason like this.

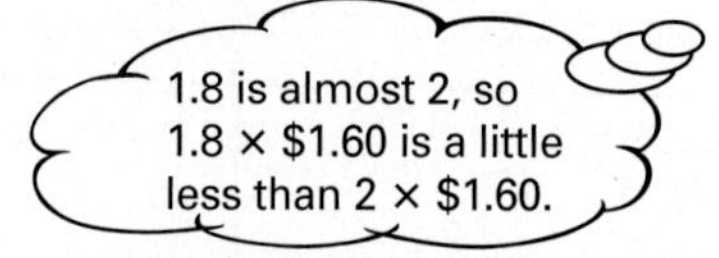

$$
\begin{aligned}
2 \times \$1.60 &= \$1.60 + \$1.60 \\
&= \$1.50 + \$0.10 + \$1.50 + \$0.10 \\
&= \$1.50 + \$1.50 + \$0.10 + \$0.10 = \$3.20
\end{aligned}
$$

$3.20 is a high estimate.

- Estimate by using simple **fractions** like halves or quarters.

You might reason like this.

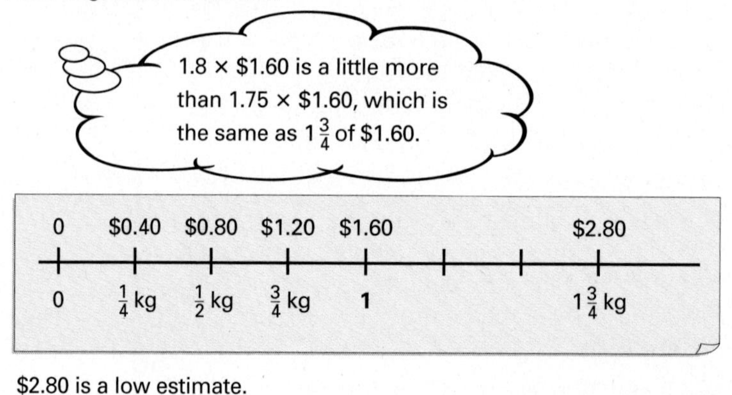

$2.80 is a low estimate.

Reaching All Learners

Parent Involvement

Have students teach their parents each of the strategies. This will help the parents to understand the strategies that have been introduced so that they can support the student's work through the rest of the curriculum.

Hints and Comments

Overview

Students read the Summary, that is continued on the next page, and discuss the different strategies they used in this section to estimate or find the cost of produce.

About the Mathematics

The Summary reviews the three main strategies developed in this section:

- rounding numbers to make them easier to work with
- converting decimals to fractions; and
- using a double number line for making an estimate

Planning

Students sometimes find it difficult to decide whether estimation is sufficient or an accurate answer is required. Discuss this with your students before they start the Check your Work problems. Also mention that sometimes estimates are used to verify the magnitude of the answer.

Produce Pricing

Notes

Be sure to go over the Check your Work problems with students so that they learn when their answer is correct, even if it does not exactly match the answer given.

1 This problem allows you to make sure that students can both read the dial scale and use reasonable estimates.

- Use an exact calculation by changing the decimals into fractions.

You might reason like this.

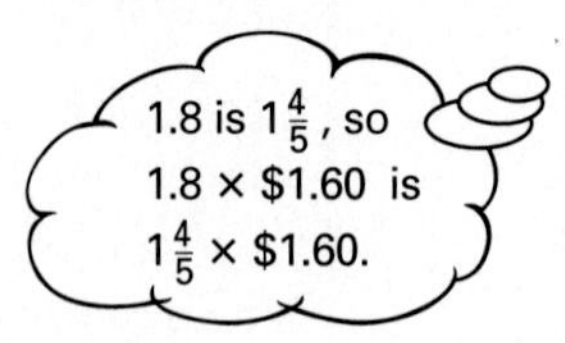

Price	\$1.60	\$0.32	\$1.28	\$2.88
Weight (kg)	1	$\frac{1}{5}$	$\frac{4}{5}$	$1\frac{4}{5}$

\$2.88 is the exact price.

- When the numbers are not easy to calculate mentally, use a calculator.

Remember: Multiplying can produce results smaller than what you start with!

Whichever method you choose, it is wise to estimate the answer before calculating. You never know when you might make an entry error or your calculator might not be working properly. It is smart to compare a reasonable estimate to your final price.

Check Your Work

At Puno's Produce, Gala apples are priced at \$2.10 per kilogram.

1. Estimate the cost of each of these amounts.

a.

b.

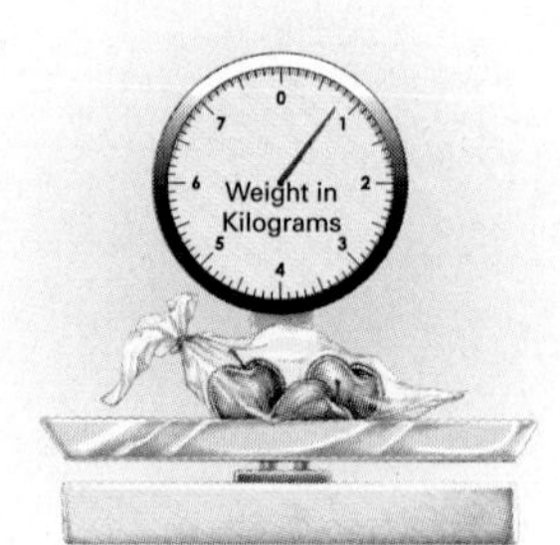

Assessment Pyramid

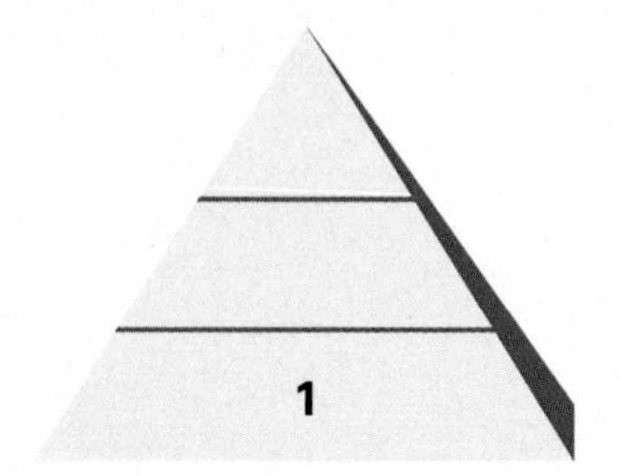

Assesses Section A Goals

Reaching All Learners

Parent Involvement

Students should share their work on these problems with their parents. Students should be able to show their parents which strategies they used for each problem.

Solutions and Samples

Answers to Check Your Work

1. a. There are different strategies to solve this problem, and there are different good solutions. However, if your answer is not between \$4.20 (= 2 × \$2.10) and \$6.30 (= 3 × \$2.10), then you should redo the problem or ask help from a classmate or your teacher.

   Sample good solutions:

   - \$5.20, because that is about halfway between \$4.20 and \$6.30.
   - \$4.62, because 2 kg of apples cost \$4.20.
     0.1 kg of apples cost \$0.21, so 0.2 kg cost \$0.42.
     2.2 kg of apples cost \$4.20 + \$0.42 = \$4.62.

   b. There are different strategies to solve this problem, and there are different good solutions. However, if your answer is not between \$1.05 (= $\frac{1}{2}$ × \$2.10) and \$2.10, then you should redo the problem or ask help from a classmate or your teacher.

   Sample good solutions:

   - \$1.50, because that is about halfway between \$1.05 and \$2.10.
   - \$1.68, because 1 kg of apples cost \$2.10.
     0.1 kg of apples cost \$0.21, so 0.2 kg cost \$0.42.
     0.8 kg of apples cost \$2.10 – \$0.42 = \$1.68.

Hints and Comments

Overview

Students continue reading the Summary. Then they can begin with the Check your Work problems.

Check Your Work

These problems are designed for student self-assessment. A student who can answer the questions correctly has understood enough of the concepts taught in the section to be able to start the next section. Students who have difficulties in answering the questions without help may need extra practice. This section is also useful for parents who want to help their children with their work. Answers are provided in the Student Book. Have students discuss their answers with classmates.

Produce Pricing

Notes

2 Some students may try to use a reverse arrow string to solve this problem. This strategy leads to division by a decimal. Students could either use a calculator or estimate by using $4 instead of $4.10.

4 If students are stuck on this problem, encourage them to think about a double number line or a ratio table.

The reflection question is meant to summarize and extend what students have learned in the section.

Produce Pricing

Paul has $7 to spend on apples.

2. How many kilograms of Gala apples can he buy?

The price of Golden Delicious apples is $3.60 per kilogram.

3. Describe how you would calculate the cost of each of these amounts of apples without using a calculator.

a. 3 kg **b.** 0.3 kg **c.** 2.3 kg

4. a. Describe how to determine $\frac{1}{2} \times \$47.00$ without using a calculator.

b. Describe how to determine $1\frac{1}{4} \times \$8.20$ without using a calculator.

Kenji used his calculator at home to calculate 12.54 × 0.39. He wrote the answer 48906 in his notebook. It wasn't until he was at school that he discovered he had forgotten to write the decimal point in his answer. He found where the decimal point should be by estimating the answer.

5. Explain what Kenji did. Place the decimal point in his answer.

For Further Reflection

Here is a multiplication problem and the correct answer, without the decimal point:

$$568 \times 356 = 202208$$

Put a decimal point in either 568, 356, or both numbers so that you will get a new multiplication problem. Be sure that your answer for the new problem is correct!

Create at least four more problems using this method.

Assessment Pyramid

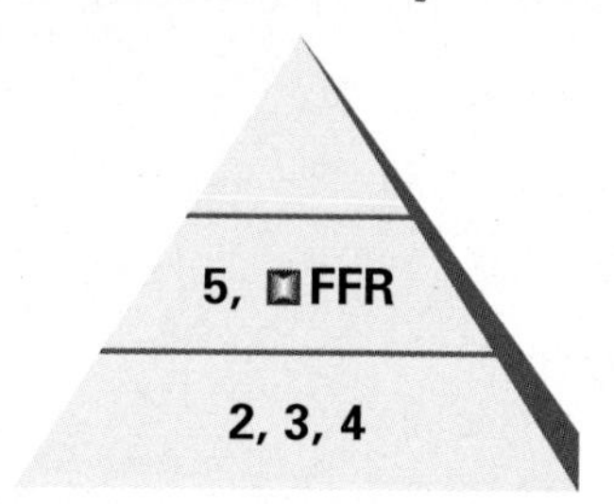

Assesses Section A Goals

Reaching All Learners

Advanced Learners

Students could be challenged to give each other problems similar to the reflection problem. They should agree on two large numbers and on the result and then take turns giving an answer with a decimal point and challenging the other to come up with the original problem. Students can also be asked how many possible problems there are for a given solution.

Solutions and Samples

2. Your answer should be a little more than 3 kg.

Sample strategy:

Three kg of apples cost \$6.30, so Paul has \$0.70 left (\$7 – \$6.30 = \$0.70).

From here, there are different strategies to continue.

- \$0.70 is about \$1, and 1 kg costs about \$2.

  \$1 out of \$2 is $\frac{1}{2}$, so he can buy about $3 + \frac{1}{2} = 3\frac{1}{2}$ kg of apples.
- One kg of apples costs \$2.10

  \$0.70 out of \$2.10 is $\frac{70}{210}$ is $\frac{1}{3}$, so he can buy $3\frac{1}{3}$ kg of apples

3. a. There are different strategies to find the price without the use of a calculator. You may have described one of the following strategies.

- Calculate the price for 3 kg using a ratio table.

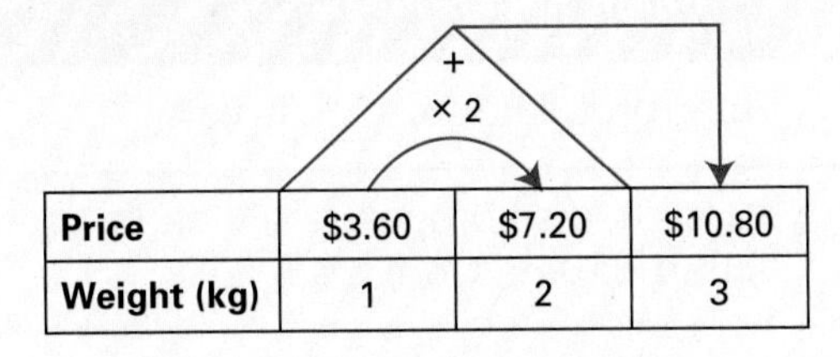

Price	\$3.60	\$7.20	\$10.80
Weight (kg)	1	2	3

- Calculate 3 × \$3.60 mentally

  3 × \$3 + 3 × \$0.60 = \$9 + \$1.80 = \$10.80

b. There are different strategies to find the price without using a calculator. You may have described the following strategy.

- In part **a**, I calculated the price for 3 kg. Since 0.3 kg is one tenth of 3 kg, I can calculate one tenth of \$10.80, which is \$1.08.

c. There are different strategies to find the price without using a calculator. You may have described the following strategy.

- In part **b**, I calculated the price for 0.3 kg (\$1.08), so I only have to add the price of 2 kg (\$7.20). The answer is \$1.08 + \$7.20 = \$8.28

4. a. $\frac{1}{2}$ × \$47.00 = \$23.50. Many strategies are possible.

Here are some.

- Separating \$47.00 as \$46.00 + \$1.00:

  $\frac{1}{2}$ of \$47.00 = $\frac{1}{2}$ of (\$46.00 + \$1.00)
  = $\frac{1}{2}$ of \$46.00 + $\frac{1}{2}$ of \$1.00
  = \$23.00 + \$0.50
  = \$23.50

Hints and Comments

Overview

Students continue working on the Check Your Work problems.

See more Hints and Comments on page 61.

- Separating \$47.00 as \$40.00 + \$7.00:

  \$47.00 is equal to \$40.00 + \$7.00.
  $\frac{1}{2}$ of \$40.00 is \$20.00 and $\frac{1}{2}$ of \$7.00 is \$3.50
  So $\frac{1}{2}$ × \$47.00
  = \$20.00 + \$3.50 = \$23.50.
- Thinking of \$47.00 as \$50.00 – \$3.00:

  $\frac{1}{2}$ of \$47.00 = $\frac{1}{2}$ of (\$50.00 – \$3.00)
  = $\frac{1}{2}$ of \$50.00 – $\frac{1}{2}$ of \$3.00
  = \$25.00 – \$1.50
  = \$23.50

b. $1\frac{1}{4}$ × \$8.20 = \$10.25. Strategies will vary.

- $\frac{1}{2}$ of \$8.20 = \$4.10, so
  $\frac{1}{4}$ of \$8.20 = \$2.05.
  So $1\frac{1}{4}$ × \$8.20
  = \$8.20 + \$2.05 = \$10.25.
- Using a ratio table:

Price	\$8.20	\$4.10	\$2.05	\$10.25
Weight (kg)	1	$\frac{1}{2}$	$\frac{1}{4}$	$1\frac{1}{4}$

5. Kenji might have thought:

- 12.54 is more than 12 and 0.39 is more than $\frac{1}{3}$. So the answer will be more than $\frac{1}{3}$ of 12, which is 4. Checking 4.8906 is more than 4.
- 12.54 is close to 12 and 0.39 is close to 0.5. So that would be like taking $\frac{1}{2}$ of 12, which is 6. Checking 4.8906 is reasonable.

For Further Reflection

Sample student response:

56.8 × 356 = 20,220.8 (estimation: 60 × 400 = 24,000)

56.8 × 35.6 = 2,022.08 (estimation: 60 × 40 = 2,400)

5.68 × 3.56 = 20.2208 (estimation: 6 × 4 = 24)

5.68 × 0.356 = 2.02208 (estimation: 6 × $\frac{1}{3}$ = 2)

0.568 × 0.356 = 0.202208 (estimation: half of 0.4 is 0.2)

Section Focus

Students use a bar chart and a pie chart to display the result of a survey. They describe the survey data using fractions and percents. Students use the relationships between benchmark percents and fractions and their number sense to solve percent problems, such as 25% of $40. They find discounts using their informal and formal knowledge of percents, fractions, and decimals. The instructional focus of Section B is to:

- **Calculate the percent of a number and**
- **Relate percents to fractions and decimals.**

Pacing and Planning

Day 4: Surveys		Student pages 11–13
INTRODUCTION	Problem 1	Interpret data from a survey.
CLASSWORK	Problems 2–4	Create and compare a pie chart and bar chart of data from a survey.
HOMEWORK	Problems 5 and 6	List percents that are easy to write as fractions.

Day 5: Percents and Fractions		Student pages 13–14
INTRODUCTION	Review homework.	Discuss relationships between benchmark fractions and percents.
CLASSWORK	Problems 7 and 8	Use benchmark fractions to calculate the percent of a number.
HOMEWORK	Problems 9–11	Solve problems involving percent discounts.

Day 6: Percents or Cents?		Student pages 14–17
INTRODUCTION	Review homework.	Review homework from Day 5.
CLASSWORK	Problems 12–13	Calculate reasonable percent discounts.
HOMEWORK	Check Your Work and For Further Reflection	Students self-assess their understanding of Section B goals.

Day 7: Reasonable Discounts		Student pages 16 and 17
INTRODUCTION	Review homework.	Review homework from Day 6.
ASSESSMENT	Quiz 1	Quiz addressing Sections A and B goals.

Additional Resources: *Number Tools,* pages 70-75; Additional Practice, Section B, page 36

Materials

Student Resources
Quantities listed are per student.

- Student Activity Sheets 1 and 2

Teachers Resources
No resources required.

Student Materials
Quantities listed are per student.

- Calculator

* See Hints and Comments for optional materials.

Learning Lines

Concepts *Percents*

In this section, various strategies are introduced to help students develop their ability to solve percent problems mentally, or with paper and pencil.

For these strategies they use:

- benchmark fractions like $\frac{1}{2}$, $\frac{1}{4}$, and $\frac{1}{10}$
- percents related to benchmark fractions, like 50%, 25%, and 10%
- the relationship between ratios, fractions, decimals, and percents
- rounding numbers to estimate percents
- the 1% and 10% strategy

For example, to find 16% of $220, students can separate the 16% into the sum of several percentages that are easier to calculate. 16% = 10% + 5% + 1%. The result is $22 + $11 + $2.20 and the answer is $35.20. Note that a ratio table can be very helpful in organizing these calculations:

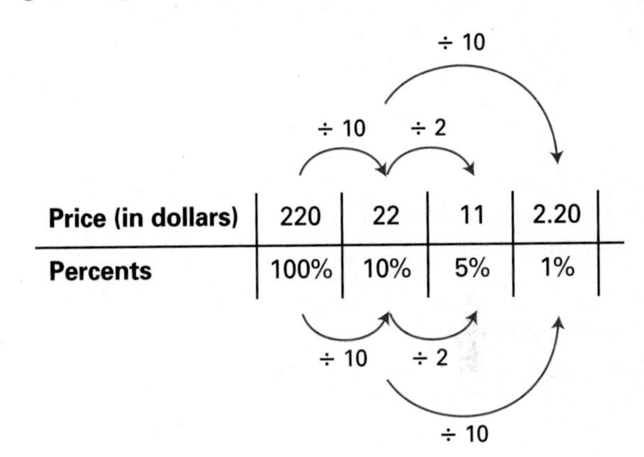

Price (in dollars)	220	22	11	2.20
Percents	100%	10%	5%	1%

Models

In this section, the use of the fraction bar, double number line, and ratio table is further developed.

At the End of This Section: Learning Outcomes

Students are able to relate percents to fractions and to decimals. They can calculate a percent of a number and discount and sale price.

Notes

1 Encourage students to use their number sense and estimation strategies. Although it is not required, students might use fractions and percents, which will be used in problem 2.

2a This is a strategy that students should be familiar with from the unit *Fraction Times*.

2b This is intended to be an approximation rather than an exact fraction.

2c Students may use their answers from problem 2b and the relationship between benchmark fractions and percents.

Discounts

Surveys

Ms.Vander of Save Supermarket replaced the old dial scales in the produce section with digital scales.

She wanted to know how the customers felt about the new scales, so she surveyed 650 customers.

The first survey question asked, "Do you like the new scales?"

Here are the results from the first survey question.

Customer Opinion of New Scales	
Number of Customers	**Customer's Opinion**
320	very pleased with the new scales
220	somewhat pleased with the new scales
65	not pleased with the new scales
The rest of the customers surveyed said they did not notice the difference.	

1. Do the customers think the new scales are a good idea? Use the survey results to explain your answer.

Ms. Vander made a pie chart to help her interpret the survey results.

2. a. Display the results using the segmented bar and pie chart on **Student Activity Sheet 1**.
   b. Describe the results of the survey using fractions.
   c. Describe the results of the survey using **percents**.

Reaching All Learners

Vocabulary Building

Students may not be familiar with the term *digital*, or may have only heard it in relation to a clock. You can ask students to explain what is meant by a digital scale by using their understanding of a digital clock.

Advanced Learner

Students could be asked what the advantages and disadvantages of a digital scale might be. One advantage is accuracy; disadvantages include the need for electricity.

Solutions and Samples

1. Answers will vary. Sample responses:

   Yes, the new scales were a good idea since a little less than half (49%) of the customers were very pleased with them.

   I think the new scales were a good idea, but Ms. Vander should be concerned that about 10% (65 out of 650) of the customers were not pleased with the new scales.

2. a.

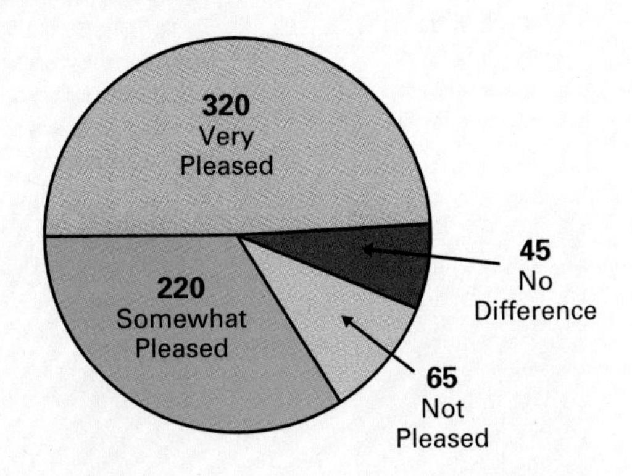

   Each of the 65 segments of the segmented bar represents ten customers. Color 32 segments for 320 people, 22 segments for 220 people, 6.5 segments for 65 people, and 4.5 segments for the remaining people. Then cut out and form the segmented bar graph into a circle to determine the size of each region in the pie chart.

   b. Close to one-half of the customers were very pleased, about one-third were somewhat pleased, one-tenth were not pleased, and about one-fifteenth did not notice the difference. Strategies will vary. Students may visually estimate the fractions using the pie chart.

   c. About 50% of the customers were very pleased, about 35% were somewhat pleased, 10% were not pleased, and about 7% did not notice the difference. Strategies will vary. Students may use a calculator, a ratio table, or a percent bar.

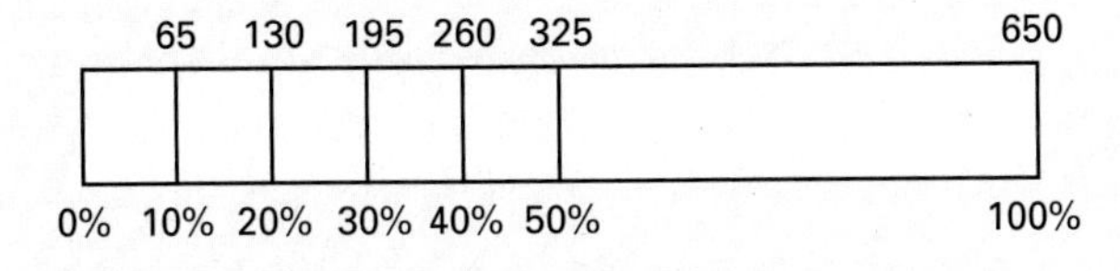

Hints and Comments

Materials

Student Activity Sheet 1 (one per student)

Overview

Students use a segmented bar graph and pie chart to describe the survey data using fractions and percents.

About the Mathematics

The segmented bar is first divided into regions that represent each of the groups of data.

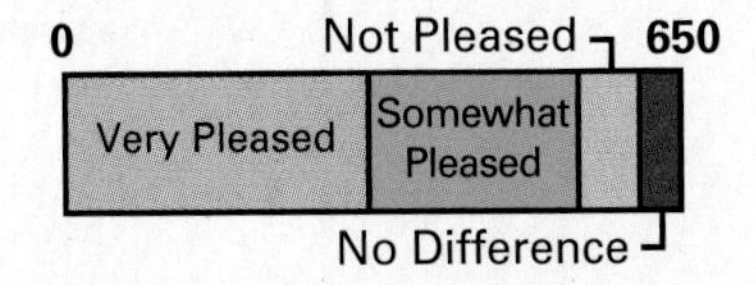

Then the bar is cut out, the ends are connected, and the now circular bar is placed over a circle to measure the proportionate regions of the pie chart.

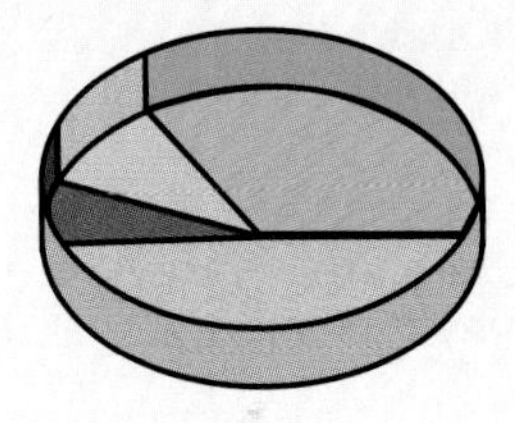

Planning

You might use problem 1 to introduce this section. Discuss surveys and how they are used. Ask students what is needed from a survey in order to draw certain conclusions. Students may compare percents or fractions to give examples of the opinions of a majority.

The Sale (discounts) activity in *Number Tools,* pages 74 and 75, can also be used for additional practice.

Comments About the Solutions

2. a. Some students may forget to compute the number of customers who did not notice the difference. (45).

Discounts

Notes

3 This problem is similar to ones in the unit *Fraction Times*. It is critical that students notice the last part of Mr. Sanchez's comment so that they understand that there are four possible survey responses.

3b Students should be able to answer in terms of fractions.

4 This problem allows students to reflect on the two different representations used so far and think about which they think is easier.

The second survey question asked, "Do the new scales help you estimate the cost of your selection?"

Ms. Vander was amazed at the results of the second survey question. She decided to show her staff members the results on a bar chart. Here are some of their reactions.

Bert Loggen
Produce Manager

Janice Vander
Store Manager

Juan Sanchez
Produce Buyer

3. a. Draw a bar chart that Ms. Vander could have shown her staff.
   b. Describe the part of the chart that represents the number of customers who say it doesn't make any difference which scale is used.

4. a. Which type of graph, the pie chart or the bar chart, makes it easier to see the parts that are larger as compared to the parts that are smaller? Explain.
   b. **Reflect** How can these charts help you figure out the percents for the parts?
   c. Can the charts help you find the fractions that describe the parts? Explain your answer.

Reaching All Learners

Intervention

It may be helpful to summarize each of the customers' comments so that all students are clear about the data before they begin problem 3.

Advanced Learners

To extend problem 3 you might ask, "How would you describe the part of the customers that say it doesn't make any difference?" (15%) Be sure to ask how the students arrived at their answer.

Solutions and Samples

3. a.

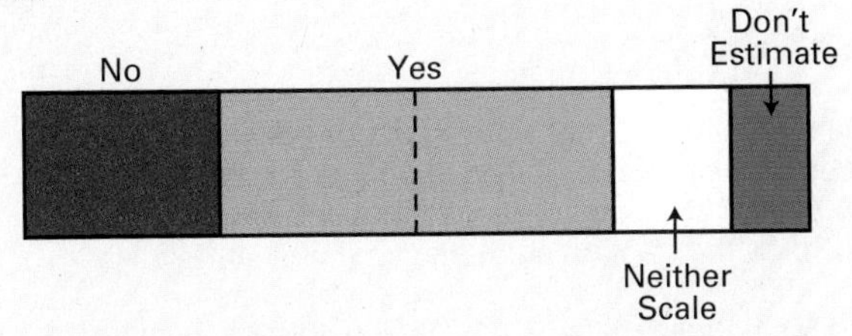

b. Answers will vary. Sample responses:

Strategy 1: Students may use percentages. Taking the percentages already mentioned, 25%, 50% (half), and 10% (one-tenth), leaves 15%. Students may answer that the section is 15%.

Strategy 2: Students may use fractions. Taking the fraction already mentioned, $\frac{1}{4}$ (25%), $\frac{1}{2}$ and $\frac{1}{10}$; added they are $\frac{17}{20}$. This leaves $\frac{3}{20}$.

4. a. Answers will vary. Sample responses:

The pie chart makes it easier to see which parts are smaller and which parts are bigger since I can compare the sizes of the slices.

The bar chart makes it easier to see which parts are smaller and which parts are bigger because I can compare the widths of the parts.

b. Answers will vary. Sample response:

I can look at the charts and estimate how much each part is of the whole and then write each as a percent.

c. Answers will vary. Sample responses:

Yes, since the charts can help me estimate the percent for each part, then all I have to do is rewrite the percent as a fraction.

Sometimes the charts can help me write the parts as fractions, especially if I can tell that one of the parts is definitely one-half or one-fourth of the whole.

Hints and Comments

Materials

transparencies of the pie chart in problem 2a and the bar chart in problem 3 (optional, one per class)

Overview

Students explain how to use the bar and pie charts to find percents and fractions that describe survey results.

About the Mathematics

Below are sample strategies students might use:

- 320 is what percent of 650? Using benchmark fractions and percents, some students might reason that it is about half, or 50%. Other students might use a percent bar.
- 45 is what percent of 650? Using the 10% strategy, some students might reason that 65 is 10% of 650 and half of 65 is about 33 or 5% of 650, so 45 is between 5% and 10%. 1% is 6.5 and 2% is 13.

  33 + 13 is about 45, so it is 5% + 2%, which is 7%.

Planning

Students can continue working in small groups on these problems. Discuss problem 3, asking students how they divided the bar into parts. Point out that this problem can be solved without knowing the actual number of customers. Problem 4 may be assigned as homework.

Bringing Math Home

Have students pose problem 4a to different family members and record their responses in their journal. Students should then solve problems 4b and 4c individually and discuss the answers with their family.

Notes

This page focuses on use of benchmark fractions to solve problems involving percents.

7 The number 364 was chosen because it is easy to work with. Since each of these problems has the same base number, students may be able to use their answers from one part to another. For example, students should see that the answer to part f is simply part a plus part c.

8 To save the time of copying all these problems it may be useful to provide a worksheet with the problems already written down. Encourage students to do the problems in an order that makes sense to think about what they are doing. This will help on the next page.

Percents and Fractions

Some store managers do not make pie charts or bar charts to show the results of customer surveys. They use only percents. Some percents, like 50% and 25%, are as easy to write as fractions. Check that you know the fraction equivalents of 50% and 25%.

Ms. Vander told Mr. Loggen that $33\frac{1}{3}$% of 180 customers wish Save Supermarket would carry a wider variety of apples. Without a calculator, Mr. Loggen quickly figured out that $33\frac{1}{3}$% of 180 customers is 60 customers.

5. What strategy do you think Mr. Loggen used to find the answer?
6. List percents that are easy to rewrite as fractions. Include the corresponding fractions.

Fractions like $\frac{1}{2}$ and $\frac{1}{4}$ and $\frac{1}{10}$ are often called **benchmark fractions.**

7. Show how you can use benchmark fractions to calculate each of these percent problems.

   a. 25% of 364
   b. 75% of 364
   c. 10% of 364
   d. 5% of 364
   e. 30% of 364
   f. 35% of 364
   g. 20% of 364
   h. 80% of 364

Dale's Department Store is having a sale. Dale wants all his employees to be able to do mental calculations quickly and easily in case customers have questions about the sale **discounts.**

8. Complete these mental calculations. You do not have to answer them in any particular order. You may want to start with those you find the easiest. Write your answers in your notebook.

   a. $\frac{15}{100}$ of $360 is ____.
   b. 35% of $360 is ____.
   c. 20% of $250 is ____.
   d. $33\frac{1}{3}$% of $120 is ____.
   e. 0.25 × $360 is ____.
   f. $\frac{1}{4}$ of $360 is ____.
   g. 25% × $360 is ____.
   h. 0.333 × $360 is ____.
   i. $\frac{1}{5}$ of $250 is ____.
   j. 1% of $250 is ____.
   k. $\frac{1}{3}$ of $360 is ____.
   l. 40% of $250 is ____.
   m. $\frac{3}{4}$ of $360 is ____.
   n. 15% of $360 is ____.

Assessment Pyramid

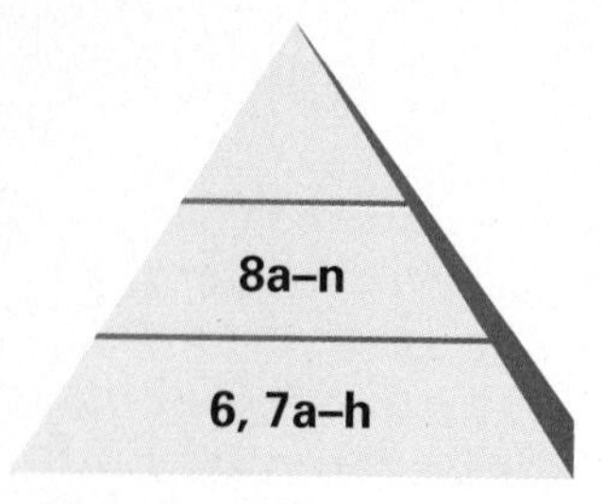

Relate percents to fractions and decimals.

Know benchmark percents. Find a percent of a number.

Reaching All Learners

Vocabulary Building

The term *benchmark fraction* is used on this page. A benchmark fraction is one that is found easily and used frequently.

Accommodation

Students may not be able to determine which percents they should know. You can provide a list of percentages and have the students fill in the fractions, or vice-versa. Students could then use this sheet as they work on the rest of the page.

Solutions and Samples

5. Answers will vary. Sample response:

   Mr. Loggen knew that $33\frac{1}{3}\%$ of a number is $\frac{1}{3}$ of that number, so he divided 180 customers by 3 to get 60 customers.

6. Answers will vary. Sample responses:

Percent	Fraction
50%	$\frac{1}{2}$
25%	$\frac{1}{4}$
75%	$\frac{3}{4}$
10%	$\frac{1}{10}$
1%	$\frac{1}{100}$
$33\frac{1}{3}\%$	$\frac{1}{3}$
20%	$\frac{1}{5}$

7. **a.** 91. Strategies will vary. Sample strategy:
   25% is half of one-half.
   One-half of 364 is 182, and half of 182 is 91.

   b. 273. Strategies will vary. Sample strategies:
   75% percent is $\frac{3}{4}$ part, so divide 364 by 4 and then multiply that answer by 3 to get 273.

   Using the answer from part a: 25% of 364 is 91 and 75% is three times as much, so $3 \times 91 = 273$.

   c. 36.4. Strategies will vary. Sample strategy:
   10% is $\frac{1}{10}$ part, and $\frac{1}{10}$ of 364 is 36.4.

   d. 18.2. Strategies will vary. Sample strategy:
   Five percent is half of 10%, so find one-half of 36.4, which is 18.2.

   e. 109.2. Strategies will vary. Sample strategy:
   $30\% = 3 \times 10\%$.
   10% of 364 is 36.4,
   30% of 364 is 3×36.4, or 109.2.

   f. 127.4. Strategies will vary. Sample strategy:

   $35\% = 30\% + 5\%$, so add the answers of problems 7e and 7d:

   $109.2 + 18.2 = 127.4$.

   g. 72.8. Strategies will vary. Sample strategy:

   Twenty percent is two times 10%,
   so $2 \times 36.4 = 72.8$.

   h. 291.2. Strategies will vary. Sample strategy:

   Since $80\% = 100\% - 20\%$, and 20% of 364 is 72.8 (from problem 7g), subtract 72.8 from 364. So, 80% of 364 is $364 - 72.8$, which is 291.2.

8. **a.** $54 **b.** $126 **c.** $50 **d.** $40 **e.** $90
   f. $90 **g.** $90 **h.** $120 **i.** $50 **j.** $2.50
   k. $120 **l.** $100
   m. $270 **n.** $54.

Hints and Comments

Materials

calculators (optional, one per student)

Overview

Students use number sense and relationships between benchmark fractions and percents to solve percent problems. Students also solve problems in which they mentally calculate the amounts of discount.

About the Mathematics

The problems on this page give students the opportunity to develop strategies to solve percent problems. The term *benchmark fraction*, refers to fractions such as $\frac{1}{2}, \frac{1}{3}, \frac{3}{4}, \frac{1}{10}, \frac{1}{100}$ that can be used to find percents. At this point, most students should understand and be able to use the relationships between percents and fractions. Students who are not yet ready to compute abstractly may use fractions or percent bars, double number lines, or ratio tables. In problem 8, students may begin to use a percent as an operator.

Planning

Discuss students' responses to problems 5 and 6 before they continue. You may want students to work on problems 7 and 8 individually.

Be sure to discuss problems 7f and h, since these problems elicit the greatest variety of strategies.

Problem 7 can be used as informal assessment and problem 8 can be assigned as homework.

Comments About the Solutions

5. Most students will recall that to calculate $\frac{1}{3}$ of a number can be done by dividing that number by 3.

7. Observe students' strategies to determine whether or not they use the same method to solve each problem or use a variety of strategies. Those who convert percents into fractions or break down a percent into a sum or benchmark percents and their corresponding fractions show an understanding of the relationships between percents and fractions.
   Examples
   - 25% is $\frac{1}{4}$ of a number and can be calculated by dividing that number by 4.
     Taking one-half of one-half is another way to get the same result.
   - 35% is 25% + 10%, so 35% of a number can be calculated by finding one-fourth and one-tenth of the number and adding the results. Or, 35% is three times 10% plus one-half of 10%.

8. Encourage students to write each problem and its corresponding answer in their notebook. Their answers may be helpful in solving problem 10.

Notes

9 Encourage students to write down the specific strategies they used to mentally calculate the answers.

11 After students complete this problem, have a whole class discussion about which problems students saw as related and about which they found easy or hard. Some students in the class might find one problem difficult while others might find the same one easy. Have students who found the problem easy share their strategies.

12 Be sure students understand that they are looking for the lower price. You may need to discuss the fact that this means they are looking for the bigger discount.

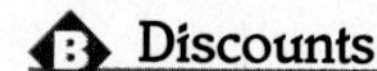

9. Choose three of your mental calculations and describe your solution strategy for each one.

10. Which of the mental calculations you used in problem 8 are related? Explain how they are related.

11. **Reflect** Which of the calculations you used in problem 8 are the easiest for you to compute mentally? Which of the calculations would you rather do using a calculator?

Percents or Cents?

During a sale, Dale offers two types of discounts. Sometimes he gives a cash discount and other times he gives a percent off the regular price.

12. a. On **Student Activity Sheet 2**, you will find a copy of the table below. For each item in the table, determine whether the percent discount or cash discount gives the lower sale price. Mark your choice on the activity sheet and give an explanation for it.

    b. Add two of your own items to the table on the activity sheet. Include the regular prices, two types of discounts, your choice, and an explanation.

Item	Regular Price	Sale Price	Explanation
In-line Skates	$55.00	• 30% off • $10.00 off	
Jeans	$23.75	• 20% off • $5.00 off	
Cell Phone	$75.00	• 25% off • $17.50 off	
Baseball Cap	$19.95	• 15% off • $3.50 off	
Sneakers	$45.95	• 20% off • $9.00 off	
Earrings	$9.95	• 40% off • $3.50 off	

Assessment Pyramid

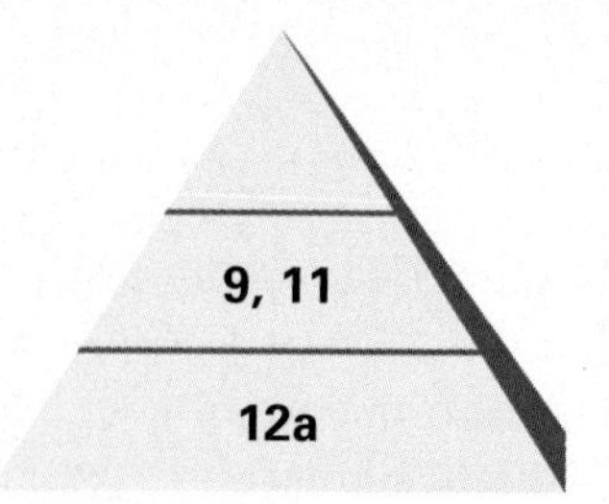

Develop number sense.

Know and use benchmark percents.

Reaching All Learners

Accommodations

Have students who have difficulty with problem 10 begin by drawing lines between the problems they think are related and then describe the relationship.

Visual Learners

Students could use a bar to show the two possible discounts in problem 12 and then make their comparison.

English Language Learners

Students might not know the names of the products listed. Each is pictured in order beside the table to support the vocabulary building.

Solutions and Samples

9. Answers will vary. Sample responses:
   - 20% of $250, I first calculated 10% of $250, which is $25, so 20% is two times as much, $50.
   - 0.333 of $360 is the same as $\frac{1}{3}$ of $360, which is $360 ÷ 3 = $120.

10. Answers will vary. Sample responses:
    - $\frac{1}{4}$ of $360, 25% of 360, and 0.25 × $360 all have the same answer. So $\frac{1}{4}$ of is the same as 25% of and the same as 0.25 ×.
    - 20% of $250 and $\frac{1}{5}$ of $250 have the same answers. So 20% of is the same as $\frac{1}{5}$ of.
    - $\frac{15}{100}$ of $360 and 15% of $360 have the same answers. So, $\frac{15}{100}$ of is the same as 15% of.

11. Answers will vary. Sample responses:

    The fraction problems were easiest to do in my head because I knew that I could divide.

    A calculator would be helpful to solve the problems that involve decimals and percents.

12. a.

Item Price	Regular Price	Sale	Explanation
In-line Skates	$55.00	☒ 30% off ☐ $10.00 off	30% off is 3 × 10%. 30% of $55 is $16.50, which is a better discount than $10 off.
Jeans	$23.75	☐ 20% off ☒ $5.00 off	10% of $23.75 is equal to about $2.37, so 20% is 2 × $2.37, which is $4.74, So, $5 off gives a better sale price.
Cell phone	$75.00	☒ 25% off ☐ $17.50 off	25% of $75 is equal to $\frac{1}{4}$ of $75, and $75 ÷ 4 is $18.75, which is a better discount than $ 17.50 off.
Baseball Cap	$19.95	☐ 15% off ☒ $3.50 off	$ 19.95 is about $20. 10% of $20 is $2. 5% of $20 is $1.00, 15% of $20 is $3. $3.50 is a better discount than 15% off.
Sneakers	$45.95	☒ 20% off ☐ $9.00 off	10% of $45.95 is about $4.60. 20% is twice that or 2 × $4.60, which is $9.20. So, 20% is a better discount than $9.00 off.
Earrings	$9.95	☒ 40% off ☐ $3.50 off	$9.95 is almost $ 10, and 40% of $10 is $4 off, which is better than $3.50 off.

b. Students may have added a variety of items to the table.

Hints and Comments

Materials

Student Activity Sheet 2 (one per student)

Overview

Students reflect on the strategies they used to solve previous problems where they calculated amounts of discount. Then students determine whether the percent discount or the dollar amount off the original prices of various items gives the better discount.

About the Mathematics

It is important that students understand that $\frac{1}{4}$ of $360 and $\frac{1}{4}$ × $360 are equivalent. Students may discover that $\frac{1}{4}$ of $360 and 0.25 × $360 are equivalent expressions.

Planning

Students may work individually on problems 9-11. Problem 9 can be used as informal assessment. Discuss students' responses to problem 10. Students may work on problem 12 in small groups, or you may want to assign this problem as homework.

Comments About the Solutions

10. Suggest that students draw lines to connect the same answers from different problems and then look for relationships among the expressions. Students may have difficulties with the number 0.333 since it is not exactly equal to $\frac{1}{3}$ and $33\frac{1}{3}$%. Since this problem involves dollar amounts, the rounded answer is equivalent to the answer of the original number divided by three.

12. Some students may use benchmark percents and their fraction equivalents to calculate answers. Others may use estimation strategies such as rounding.

Remind students to make up two additional problems and write them in the empty spaces at the bottom of the chart. Encourage them to create problems in which the percent discounts and dollar amounts are close enough to make the problems interesting. You might suggest that students first choose an item and make up its regular price. They should then choose a percent discount, such as 10%. They should then calculate the discount and use the answer to choose a dollar amount that is close to the percent discount amount.

Extension

Have students exchange papers with another student and solve each other's made-up problems from problem 12.

B Discounts

Notes

Be sure students understand the context on this page. First they need to understand that the wholesale price is the price Dale had to pay to purchase the item. The regular price is the price he normally charges. Then students need to understand that he wants to know which discounts, 10%, 25%, and/or 40%, he can give and still make money. In order to make money the sale price must remain larger than the wholesale price.

This is the first time that students are asked to calculate the sale price. At this point students are expected to calculate the discount and then subtract from the regular price.

Reasonable Discounts

13. Dale's Department Store is having a 24-hour sale. For each of the items below, the regular price is given along with the wholesale price (the price Dale's Department Store paid for the item). In each case, decide whether a discount of 10%, 25%, or 40% is reasonable. Reasonable, in this case, means a discount will provide savings for the customer but will also give the store some profit. Mark the **sale price** for each item in your notebook and defend your decision.

Assessment Pyramid

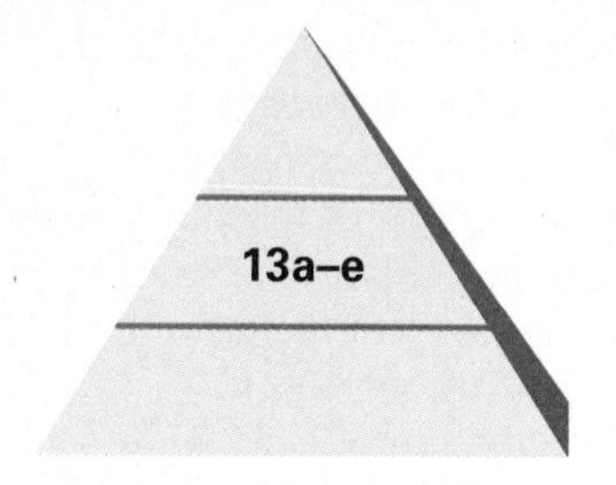

Develop number sense.

Reaching All Learners

Intervention

Students may need to be told to round the prices to the nearest dollar or even ten dollars.

Visual Learners

Students might benefit from using a double number line or bar model. Either could show all three possible discounts as well as the wholesale price.

Accommodation

With all of the information on this page, some teachers suggest making a copy of this page for students to complete their work.

Solutions and Samples

13. Strategies will vary. Sample strategy:

Round the regular price to the nearest dollar. Next, calculate 10%, 25%, and 40% of the regular price, and then subtract each one from the regular price to find the sale price. Finally, compare each sale price to the wholesale price.

a. $59.95 rounds to $60.

10% of $60 = $6, so $60 – $6 = $54

25% of $60 = $15, so $60 – $15 = $45

40% of $60 = $24, so $60 – $24 = $36

The 10% and 25% discounts are reasonable, since the wholesale price is $42.50.

b. $149.95 rounds to $150.

10% of $150 = $15, so $150 – $15 = $135

25% of $150 =$37.50, so $150 –$37.50=$112.50

40% of $150 = $60, so $150 – $60 = $90

Only the 10% discount is reasonable, since the wholesale price is $129.95.

c. $25.95 rounds to $26.

10% of $26 = $2.60, so $26 – $2.60 = $23.40

25% of $26 = $6.50, so $26 – $6.50 = $19.50

40% of $26 = $10.40, so $26 – $10.40 = $15.60

The 10% and 25% discounts are reasonable, since the wholesale price is $18.00.

d. $109.99 rounds to $110.

10% of $110 = $11, so $110 – $11 = $99

25% of $110 = $27.50, so $110 –$27.50 =$82.50

40% of $110 = $44, so $110 – $44 = $66

The 10% and 25% discounts are reasonable, since the wholesale price is $70.00.

e. Regular price is $45.

10% of $45= $4.50, so $45 – $4.50 = $40.50

25% of $45 = $11.25, so $45 – $11.25 = $33.75

40% of $45 = $18, so $45 – $18 = $27

Only the 10% discount is reasonable, since the wholesale price is $40.00. Note: Some students may say that all three percent discounts are unreasonable since the 25% and 40% discounts are both less than the wholesale price and the 10% discount is barely profitable.

Hints and Comments

Materials

calculators (optional, one per student)

Overview

Students solve more discount problems using the relationships among fractions, decimals, and percents.

Students calculate reasonable percent discount rates for various store items that give savings to customers and give some profit to the store's owner.

Planning

Discuss the terms *wholesale price* (the amount the item costs the store) and *retail* or *regular price* (the amount the customer pays without any discounts). Students may work in small groups on problem 13, or you may assign this problem as homework. Discuss students' strategies for one or two problems. Ask students if rounding the wholesale and regular prices before calculating discount rates will give accurate results on which they could base their decisions.

Comments about the Solutions

13. Most students will round the wholesale and regular prices before calculating the percent discounts. Students can solve this problem by using different strategies to calculate the percent discounts. Some students may first calculate 10% of the regular price, for example, and then calculate the sale price in this case and compare it with the wholesale price. If the result is not lower than the wholesale price, the next higher percent of discount can be calculated, and so on. An example of this strategy is shown in the solutions for problem 13a.

Other students may first calculate the difference between the regular price and the wholesale price. For example, in 13d, $110.00 – $70.00 is $40. They then determine the dollar amount deducted from the regular price for each discount. Discounts are reasonable if the dollar amount deducted is less than $40.00.

Some students may use yet another strategy from the unit *Fraction Times*. Applying this strategy to problem 13e, students first find the difference between the regular price and the wholesale price, which in this case is $5. They then write a fraction with this number and the regular price ($\frac{5}{45}$). Using a calculator, this fraction can be converted to a decimal, which is (0.11). This decimal equals $\frac{11}{100}$ or 11%. So any percent discount below 11% is reasonable for problem 13e.

B Discounts

Notes

The Summary formalizes the ideas from the section. Be sure to highlight the strategy of breaking down a difficult percent into the sum of two benchmarks. Students should have used the strategy in the section but may not have thought carefully about what they were doing. Be sure that students understand the ratio table at the bottom of the page. This is a strategy that students should be familiar with.

B Discounts

Summary

- Results of a survey can be displayed in a bar chart or a pie chart. These charts help you compare the parts using **percents** or fractions.
- **Discounts** are often expressed in percents. The strategy you use when finding discounts depends on the percent and the price given.

  Some percents, like 10%, 25%, and 75%, can easily be written as fractions. These fractions can then be used to make the calculations. For example:

  25% of 488 is $\frac{1}{4}$ of 488, which is 122.

  75% of 488 is $\frac{3}{4}$ of 488, which is 366.

Fractions that are easy to work with are called **benchmark fractions**. You can calculate with these fractions mentally.

For discounts that are not easy to compute, you can separate the percentage into the sum of several percents that are easier to calculate, such as 10% or 1%. The use of a percent bar, a double number line, or a ratio table can be helpful.

For example, to calculate 35% of $250, you can use 10% + 10% + 10% + 5% (half of 10%), or 3 × 10% + 5% (half of 10%).

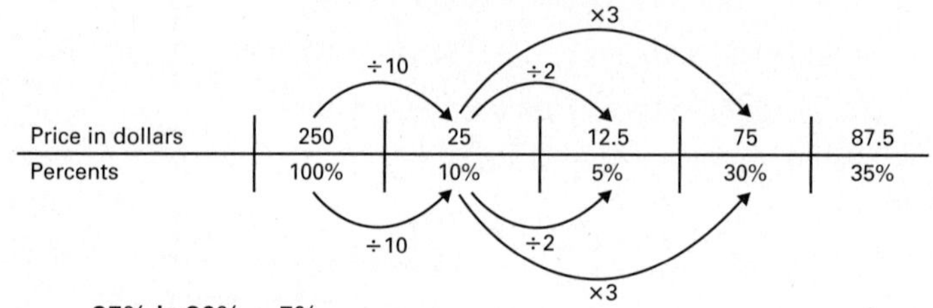

Price in dollars	250	25	12.5	75	87.5
Percents	100%	10%	5%	30%	35%

35% is 30% + 5%

3 × 10% + half of 10%

Since 10% of $250 is $25 and half of $25 is $12.50,

35% of $250 is 3 × $25 + $12.50 or

$75 + $12.50 or $87.50.

Reaching All Learners

Parent Involvement

Have students reread the Summary with their parents. Students can question their parents about which fraction percentage equivalences they know and use. They could also ask if parents ever use the strategy of adding percentages. Some parents may use this strategy to calculate a 15% tip.

Hints and Comments

Overview

Students read the Summary, which reviews the different strategies used to calculate a percent of an amount: using fractions, decimals, or the 10% and 1% strategy.

B Discounts

Notes

Have students share their strategies for these problems. There are many ways to approach them and it is important for students to see different approaches. This will also help students to see that their solution may differ from the one given and still be correct.

3 Encourage students to use different strategies in solving this problem. Challenge students to use the strategies discussed in problem 2 to find the discount prices of these three air conditioners.

4 Be sure students understand that Ms. Vander and Mr. Sanchez are going to start to solve the problem by using what they are thinking.

For Further Reflection

Reflective questions are meant to summarize concepts taught.

Check Your Work

Dale is having a sale on small fans that regularly cost $5.98 each. Customers can choose from these three discounts.

Discount 1: 5% off   Discount 2: $0.50 off

Discount 3: $\frac{1}{5}$ off

1. Which discount gives the lowest sale price? Explain your reasoning.

Dale is selling all the air conditioners in his store to make room for other merchandise. He gives his customers a huge discount of 60%.

2. Explain how you would find the discount for an air conditioner that costs $240.

Dale has three other air conditioners to sell for $280, $200, and $275.

3. How much will each one cost after the 60% discount?

Ms. Vander and Mr. Sanchez are studying a survey of 800 customers. The survey shows that 45% of the customers gave the same response. Ms. Vander and Mr. Sanchez want to know how many customers that is. They begin by using percents they can easily write as fractions.

4. How do you think Ms. Vander and Mr. Sanchez will continue? Complete their calculations.

5. Write at least two ways to calculate 25% of 900.

For Further Reflection

Look for at least three different sale items listed in a newspaper or magazine. Calculate the discount and the sale price. Rewrite the percent discount as a fraction.

Assessment Pyramid

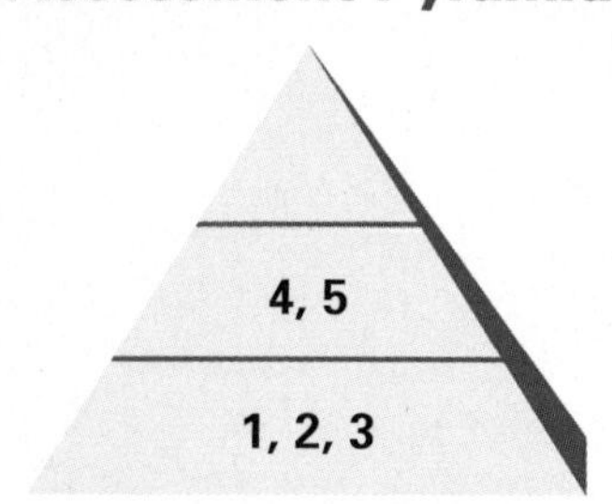

Assesses Section B Goals

Reaching All Learners

Parent Involvement

Students should share their work with their parents. They can work with their parents to complete the For Further Reflection problem.

Extension

Ask students, "How would you compare the answers to 20% of 35 and 35% of 20?" (The answer is 7 in each case.) How would you compare the answers to 25% of 84 and 84% of 25? (The answer is 21 in each case.) Ask students, "What problem is related to 15% of 40?" (40% of 15.) Have students write a rule for these related percent problems. (Sample response: Related percent problems have the same answer. You can switch the numbers in related percent problems and still get the same answer.)

Solutions and Samples

Answers to Check Your Work

1. Discount 3 gives the best sale price. You may have used one of the following strategies:

   - Calculate and compare the discount prices.

     Discount 1: 10% of \$5.98 is about \$0.60. So 5% of \$5.98 is about \$0.30.

     The sale price is \$5.98 – \$0.30 = \$5.68.

     Discount 2: The discount is \$0.50 off. So the sale price is \$5.98 – \$0.50 = \$5.48.

     Discount 3: One-fifth of \$5.98 is about \$1.20. So the sale price is \$5.98 – \$1.20 = \$4.78.

     So Discount 3 gives the best sale price (largest discount).

   - Calculate and compare the discount fractions.

     Discount 1: 5% off is $\frac{1}{20}$ off.

     Discount 2: \$0.50 off of \$6.00 is
     $\frac{50}{600} = \frac{5}{60} = \frac{1}{12}$.
     Discount 3: $\frac{1}{5}$ off
     $\frac{1}{5}$ is greater than $\frac{1}{20}$ and $\frac{1}{12}$.
     So Discount 3 gives the best sale price.

   - Use percents to compare the discounts:

     Discount 1: 5%

     Discount 2: \$0.50 is a bit less than 10% of \$5.98.

     Discount 3: $\frac{1}{5}$ is 20%.

     So Discount 3 gives the best sale price.

2. The discount is \$144. You may have used one of the following strategies.

   - Thinking of 60% as 50% + 10%:

     Use a percent bar.

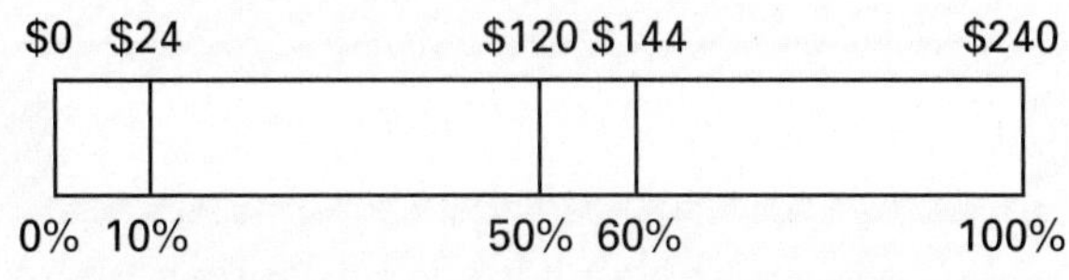

     Since 60% can be written as 50% + 10%, find 50% of \$240, which is equal to \$120.

     Then find 10% of \$240, which is equal to \$24.

     So 60% of \$240 = \$120 + \$24 = \$144.

   - Thinking of 60% as six 10%s:

     Since 60% can be written as six 10%s, find 10% of \$240, which is equal to 24.

     Then multiply 24 by 6, which is equal to 144.

     So 60% of \$240 = \$144.

   - Using a calculator:

     Enter: 0.60 × 240 = 144.

3. The \$280 air conditioner will cost \$112; the \$200 air conditioner will cost \$80; the \$275 air conditioner will cost \$110. You may have used the following strategy.

   \$280 air conditioner:
   60% of \$280 = \$168.
   The sale price is \$280 – \$168 = \$112.

   \$200 air conditioner:
   60% of \$200 = \$120.
   The sale price is \$200 – \$120 = \$80.

   \$275 air conditioner:
   60% of \$275 = \$165.
   The sale price is \$275 – \$165 = \$110.

4. **a.** There are different ways to finish their calculations. You may have used one of these strategies.

   - Ms. Vander uses $\frac{1}{10}$ of 800 = 80:
     $\frac{1}{10}$ of 800 = 80, and
     4 × 80 = 40% of 800 = 320. Also,
     since 10% of 800 = 80, 5% is equal to one-half of 80, which is 40.
     So 45% of 800 = 320 + 40 = 360.

   - Ms. Vander could have also used a 10% strategy:

     10% of 800 is 80, so 40% is 320 (4 × 80).
     5% is half of 10%, so 5% is 40 ($\frac{1}{2}$ × 80).
     So 45% is 360 (320 + 40).

   - Mr. Sanchez uses a 45% is 50% – 5% strategy:

     50% is 400 ($\frac{1}{2}$ of 800). I need to take off 5%.
     5% is 40 ($\frac{1}{10}$ of 50%).
     45% is 360 (400 – 40).

     Or using a ratio table:

Number of Customers	800	400	40	360
Percent	100%	50%	5%	45%

5. Answers will vary. Sample responses:

   - Half of 50% is 25%.
     50% of 900 is 450 ($\frac{1}{2}$ of 900).
     Half of 50% is 225.
     25% is $\frac{1}{4}$ of the whole.
     I can find $\frac{1}{4}$ of 900 by dividing 900 by four;
     900 ÷ 4 = 225.

For Further Reflection

You may have students share and discuss their work in small groups.

See Hints and Comments on page 62.

Section Focus

Students draw percent bars to illustrate discounts and sale prices. They use fractions and percents to express the relationship among regular price, sale price, and discount. Students solve problems about increase and decrease; the changes are indicated by fractions and by percentages. They start to develop the multiplicative strategy to solve this type of problems. This strategy is further developed in Section D. The instructional focus of Section C is to:

- **use percent bars to solve problems involving percents;**
- **calculate total cost with tax; and**
- **determine original price given the sale price and percent discount.**

Pacing and Planning

Day 8: Design a Sign		Student pages 18–19
INTRODUCTION	Problems 1 and 2	Sketch signs that describe produce discounts.
CLASSWORK	Problems 3–5	Represent percent discounts using percent bars.
HOMEWORK	Problem 6	Use one multiplication to find a sale price.

Day 9: Profit Fractions		Student pages 20–22
INTRODUCTION	Problems 7 and 8	Identify fractional change in profit.
CLASSWORK	Problems 9–12	Calculate change in profit using fractions and percents.
HOMEWORK	Problems 13 and 14	Calculate the sale price of grocery items.

Day 10: Profit Fractions (continued)		Student pages 22–25
INTRODUCTION	Problem 15	Solve problems involving percent increase and percent decrease.
CLASSWORK	Problems 16–18	Investigate common misconceptions of percent increase and decrease.
HOMEWORK	Check Your Work and For Further Reflection	Students self-assess their understanding of Section C goals.

Day 11: Summary		Student pages 24 and 25
INTRODUCTION	Review homework and read Summary	Review homework from Day 10.
ASSESSMENT	Quiz 2	Quiz addressing Section A through C goals.

Additional Resources: *Number Tools* resource, pages 46-50; Additional Practice, Section C, page 37

Materials

Student Resources

Quantities listed are per student.

- **Student Activity Sheets 3, 4, and 5**

Teachers Resources

No resources required.

Student Materials

Quantities listed are per student.

- Calculator

* See Hints and Comments for optional materials.

Learning Lines

Models

The percent bar is a model that is developed in the *Mathematics in Context* curriculum to represent and make sense of calculations and problems involving percents. Because the percent bar is a visual model, students reason and justify calculations by relating the model to the context of the problem.

Concepts *Percents*

In this section, students use the percent bar to represent percent increase and decrease in the price of an item.

For example, decrease:

Suppose an item is discounted by 25%.

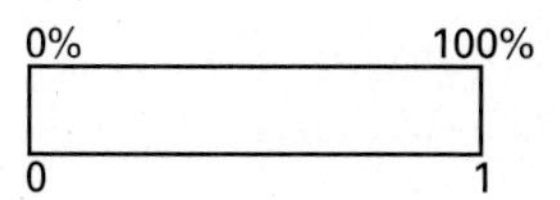

Students can find the sale price using the relationship between percents and fractions: the discount is 25% or $\frac{1}{4}$; calculate $\frac{1}{4}$ of the price and subtract this to find the sale price.

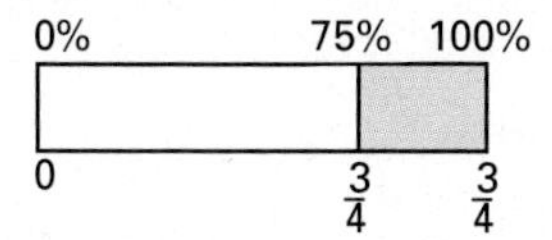

This strategy is named the *additive strategy*.

The *multiplicative strategy*:

The discount is 25%, so the sale price is 75% of the original price. You can multiply $\frac{3}{4}$ times the original price to get the sale price.

This multiplication strategy will be developed further in section D.

At the End of this Section: Learning Outcomes

Students will be able to calculate the sale price of an item with a discount given as a percent or fraction. Students solve problems involving decrease and increase and they use the relationship between benchmark fractions and percents. They start to use advanced multiplication strategies to find a percent discount.

Many Changes

Notes

In the previous section, students calculated some discounts. However, this section formalizes strategies for solving discount problems.

1 This problem is intended to get students to think about what the various discounts mean. Student responses should be informal.

3a Students' answers to this question give you some insight into how comfortable they are with fractions and percentages.

Many Changes

Design a Sign

Save Supermarket is planning a super sale. They want to design a sale sign showing the produce prices. Ms. Vander gives these discounts.

Grapes
Were \$3.20/kg
Now 25% off

Granny Smith Apples
Were \$2.89/kg
Now 20% off

Red Delicious Apples
Were \$2.40/kg
Now 15% off

1. Are these good sales for customers?

The employees brainstorm about what to write on the sale signs.

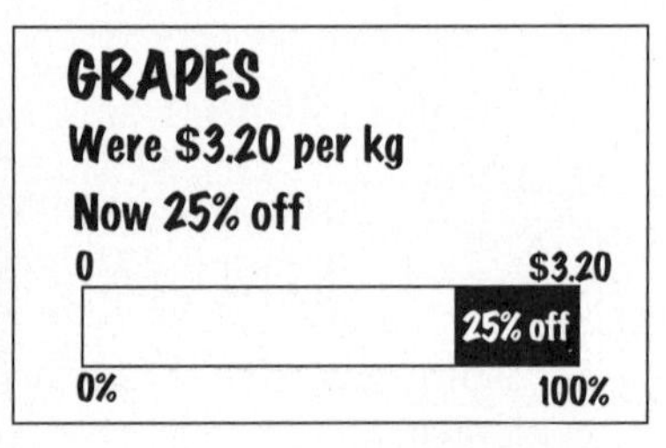

Bert sketched this sign for grapes. He used a percent discount and a **percent bar** to visually show the relationship between the original price and the discount price.

2. Sketch signs for Granny Smith and Red Delicious apples using Bert's suggestions.

Janice proposes that they include fractions instead of percents. She believes customers can estimate the discounts more easily if they use fractions.

3. a. **Reflect** Do you agree with Janice? Defend your position.
   b. Draw one sign using Janice's suggestion.

Reaching All Learners

Advanced Learners

Students can be challenged to pick the Red Delicious apples for 3b since that is not a benchmark fraction.

Writing Opportunity

Ask students to write in their journal about a personal experience in which they bought something at a particularly good sale price. Have them write about how much they saved and how it made them feel.

Solutions and Samples

1. Answers will vary. Some students may recall sales in the stores where they shop and believe this is about average for sales. Others may think that since the discounts are all less than $1 off, the sales are not very good.

   Discount on Grapes: $0.80
   Discount on Granny Smith apples: $0.58
   Discount on Red Delicious apples: $0.36

2.

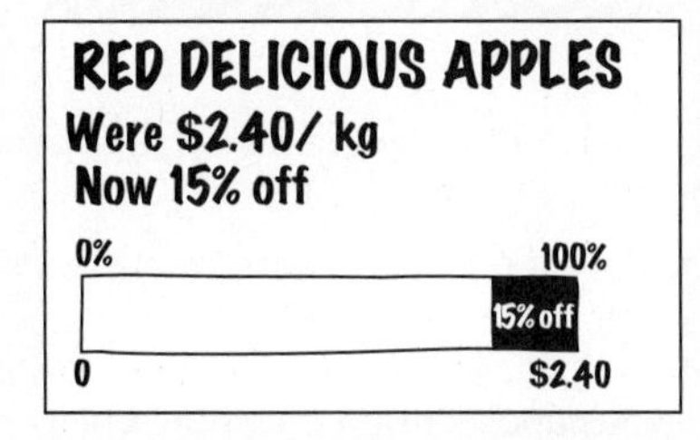

3. **a.** Answers will vary. Some students may agree with Janice, saying that when they compute a percent, they always change the percent into a fraction and find a fraction of the price.

   Others may disagree with Janice because they use another strategy, such as the 10% or 1% strategy, to figure percents.

   b. Answers will vary. Sample response:

GRAPES

Were $3.20/kg

Now $\frac{1}{4}$ off the price!

Hints and Comments

Overview

Students compare percent discounts for different fruits and vegetables and draw percent bars to illustrate the amount of discount in each case. They start to express percent discounts as fractions.

About the Mathematics

In this section, the percent bar is used as a tool to visualize the mathematical structure of discount problems rather than as a model to support computations. It depicts that, given a discount of P%, the sale price is (100 – P)% of the original price. Students will develop this strategy in problems 1–5 and use it formally in problem 6.

For example, this bar shows that, given 25% off the original price, the sale price is 75% of the original price. Also the relationship between percents and fractions can be illustrated with a bar:

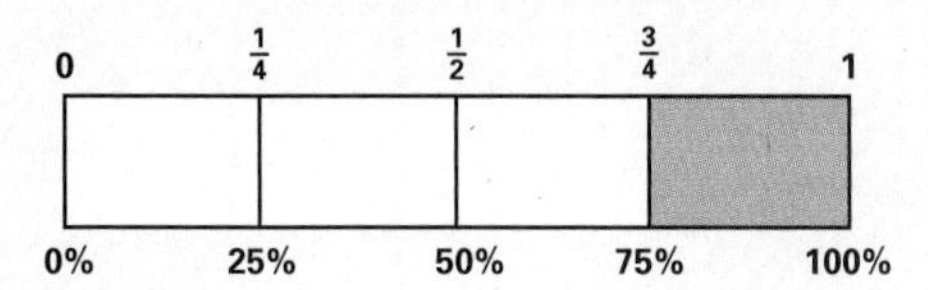

Planning

Students may work in small groups on these problems to facilitate group discussions. The Percent Bars activity on pages 46 and 47 of the *Number Tools* resource can be used here for additional practice.

Comments About the Solutions

1. This problem gives students an opportunity to explore the meaning of the percents in relation to the prices.

2. Students may remember from previous Number units that dividing bars into equal parts can help them estimate what part or parts should be shaded. Discuss this concept with students.

3. **b.** Students will probably choose to make a sign for the product whose percent is easiest to convert to a fraction. You might ask students how they could convert 15% to a fraction. (Write 15% as $\frac{15}{100}$; Then reduce that to $\frac{3}{20}$.)

Notes

4 Students can be required to answer this problem in a variety of ways. It can be a small group or whole class discussion, a short answer, a pros-and-cons list, or a formal paragraph.

6a Have students share their strategies for this problem. Focus the discussion on the relationship between $\frac{3}{4}$ of \$3.20 and $\frac{3}{4} \times$ \$3.20. Ask students for strategies for making the calculation, with and without a calculator. Some students may still multiply $\frac{1}{4} \times$ \$3.20 and then subtract the discount amount from the original price. Allow this strategy but as the unit progresses encourage students to multiply the original price by the percent of the sale price.

Ms. Vander is in favor of displaying the discount in dollars.

Pedro thinks it will be easier for customers if only the new price appears on the signs.

4. What kind of sign do you prefer? Why?

The employees decide to combine ideas. They will use a percent bar, the percent discount, and both the original price and the sale price on each sign.

5. Use their ideas to design new signs for each of the items on the left.

Pedro studies the new grapes sign and says, "This is great! You can tell just by looking at the sign what fraction or percent the customers will have to pay. You can check the sale price by doing one simple multiplication."

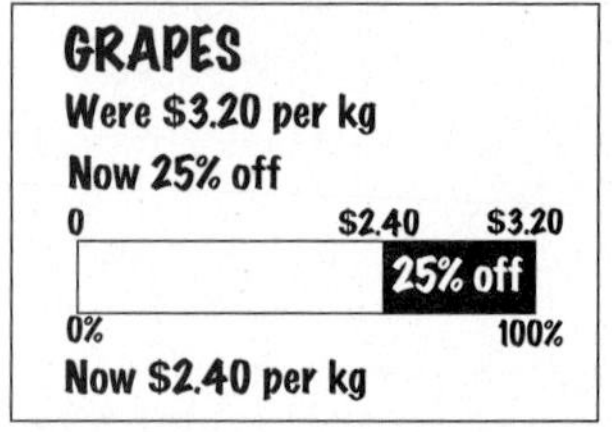

6. a. What fraction and percent of the original price do customers have to pay for grapes?

b. What multiplication can customers use to check the sale price for grapes?

c. Compute the new prices for the Granny Smith and Red Delicious apples using only one multiplication for each.

Assessment Pyramid

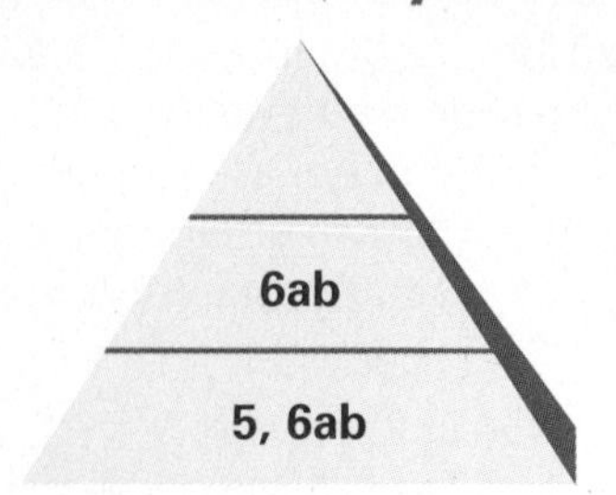

Relate percents to fractions and decimals.

Calculate sale price.

Know benchmark percents.

Reaching All Learners

Intervention

It may be helpful to have students list everything that needs to be on each of the signs before they start constructing the signs. Students could then use their list to fill in all of the information so that they have it organized before they begin to draw.

Writing Opportunity

After the class discussion of students' responses to problem 4, have students defend their position in a paragraph that they write in their journal.

Solutions and Samples

4. Answers will vary. Some students agree with Pedro, saying that just posting the new price is sufficient for a customer. Others may argue that showing the size of the discount is better for the store if the discount is sizable, so a sign listing the percent or fraction off would be important. Still others may say that it makes more of an impression on people if they can see a picture of their discount, so they would recommend using a bar chart.

5. Answers will vary.

   However, every sign should have a bar, the percent discount, and the new sale price. Sample response:

   GRAPES
   Were \$3.20/kg Now 25% off
   Sale Price
   \$2.40/kg

   GRANNY SMITH APPLES
   Were \$2.89/kg Now 20% off
   Sale Price
   \$2.31/kg

   RED DELICIOUS APPLES
   Were \$2.40/kg Now 15% off
   Sale Price
   \$2.04/kg

6. **a.** Customers have to pay $\frac{3}{4}$, or 75%, of the original price. Strategies will vary. Sample strategies:
   - The discount is 25% or $\frac{1}{4}$ of the price, so you have to pay the part that is left, which is $1 - \frac{1}{4}$ or $\frac{3}{4}$ of the original price.
   - The picture shows 25% taken from 100%, so 100% − 25% = 75%.

   b. $\frac{3}{4} \times \$3.20$ or $0.75 \times \$3.20$

   c. Granny Smith: \$2.31/kg

   Red Delicious: \$2.04/kg

   Strategies will vary. Sample strategy:

   Granny Smith apples: 20% off means that the customer pays 80% of the original price; 80% of \$2.89 can be calculated with $0.80 \times \$2.89 = \$2.31$.

   Red Delicious apples: 15% off means that the customer pays 85% of the original price; 85% of \$2.40 can be calculated with $0.85 \times \$2.40 = \$2.04$.

Hints and Comments

Materials

calculators (optional, one per student)

Overview

Students express percent discounts as fractions. They design signs that include a bar chart, the percent discount, and the new sale price on each sign.

Students express the sale price as a fraction or as a percent of the original price. They calculate the sale price by using one-step multiplication.

About the Mathematics

Students usually find the discount amount and then subtract the discount amount from the original price. In these problems students will subtract the percent discount from 100% first and then find the discount price by doing one multiplication. The outcomes will be the same, and students may find that subtracting the percents is easier than subtracting dollar amounts.

For example:

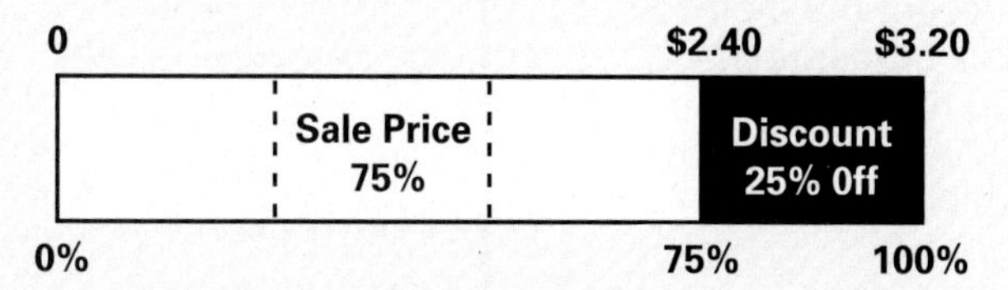

The sale price can be calculated in a one-step multiplication: $\frac{3}{4} \times$ the original price ($\frac{3}{4} \times \$3.20$), or $0.75 \times$ the original price ($0.75 \times \$3.20$).

Students must realize that the sum of the sale price and the amount of discount is the original price, so the percent that represents the sale price plus the percent discount totals 100%. Bar charts can help students make this connection. Students should be able to calculate 75% (and other benchmark percents) of an amount using the relationships between percents and fractions or decimals. Students should already know how to calculate a fraction of an amount.

Planning

Students may work on these problems in small groups. Use problems 3a and 4 to discuss which kind of sign students prefer. After students have finished problem 6, discuss it in class.

Comments About the Solutions

5. Students can revise the signs they made for problem 2 to complete this activity. Students may use segmented bars to help them estimate what part of the bars should be shaded. This was done in the unit *Fraction Times*.

Profit Fractions

The owner of Save Supermarket, Ms. Jao, compared this year's **profits** to last year's profits. This is what she found.

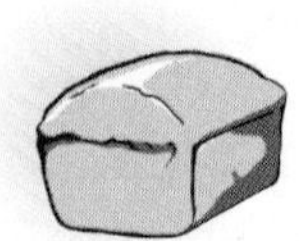

Department	Change in Profit
Health and Beauty	One-quarter less
Dairy	One-fifth less
Produce	One-and-one-half times as much
Bakery	Three-tenths less
Meat	One-quarter more
Deli	Two-thirds more

To help her visualize the changes in profits, Ms. Jao used bars to represent last year's profits.

7. a. Which departments increased profit from last year to this year?
   b. Use the bars on **Student Activity Sheet 3** to indicate the change in profit for each department. Label the bars.

This year's Health and Beauty profit can be described as three-fourths times ($\frac{3}{4}$ ×) last year's profit.

8. Describe the change in profit for the other departments in fractions.

The table below shows last year's profit for each department of Ms. Jao's store.

Department	Last Year's Profit
Health and Beauty	$46,800
Dairy	$35,600
Produce	$22,500
Bakery	$55,900
Meat	$60,200
Deli	$47,100

9. For each department, use last year's profit and the change in profit to find this year's profit.

7a It is important that students realize which are increases because these are more challenging to draw using a bar model.

7b Challenge students to think about ways to represent the increase. Some students may need hints to realize that they will have to add to the bar.

8 Encourage students to express an increase of one-fourth as $1\frac{1}{4}$ times.

9 Students may compute profits in a variety of ways. Some may change the fractions into decimals and use a calculator to multiply; others may use number sense to figure the answers.

Reaching All Learners

Intervention

Ask students to express *one-and-a-half times as much* as a fraction. Students should be able to express this as $1\frac{1}{2}$ times. Remind them that this is a direct translation of language into symbols, and this might help students to solve the other increase problems.

English Language Learners

The terms *less, more,* and *as much* can cause difficulty. Be sure to check with students after problem 7a to be sure they know which are increases and which are decreases.

Solutions and Samples

7. a. Produce, Meat, Deli.

b. Answers will vary. Sample response:

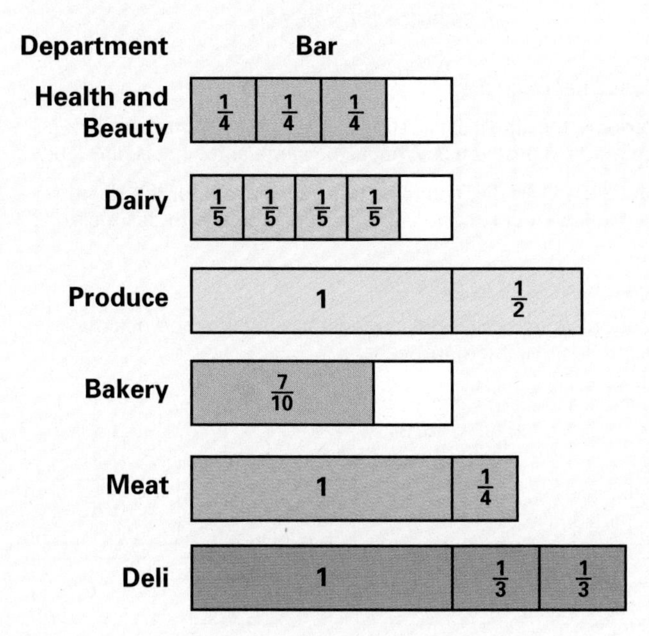

8.

Health and Beauty: $\frac{3}{4}$ × last year's profit

Dairy: $\frac{4}{5}$ × last year's profit

Produce: $1\frac{1}{2}$ × last year's profit

Bakery: $\frac{7}{10}$ × last year's profit

Meat: $1\frac{1}{4}$ × last year's profit

Deli: $1\frac{2}{3}$ × last year's profit

9.

Health and Beauty:	$35,100
Dairy:	$28,480
Produce:	$33,750
Bakery:	$39,130
Meat:	$75,250
Deli:	$78,500 (if calculated using $1\frac{2}{3}$); $78,657 (if calculated using 1.67)

Strategies will vary. Sample strategies:

Health and Beauty: $\frac{1}{4}$ × 46,800 = $11,700;

$\frac{3}{4}$ × 46,800 = 3 × $11,700 = $35,100

Dairy: 0.80 × $35,600 = $28,480

Produce: $1\frac{1}{2}$ × $22,500 = 1.5 × $22,500 = $33,750

Bakery: $\frac{7}{10}$ × $55,900 = $39,130

Meat: Multiply 1.25 × $60,200 with a calculator.

The profit for the meat department is $75,250.

Deli: $1\frac{2}{3}$ × $47,100 = $\frac{5}{3}$ × $47,100 = $78,500.

Hints and Comments

Materials

Student Activity Sheet 3 (one per student); calculators (one per student)

Overview

Students draw bar charts to show changes in profit for different departments in a grocery store from one year to the next. Students describe the changes in terms of fractions and then calculate the profit in dollar amounts.

About the Mathematics

Before this point, the percent changes in this section have been limited to percent discounts or decreases. On this page, students begin to work with increase. The change in profit is indicated by fractions. At the end of this section the changes are indicated with percentages.

Students first illustrate the profit changes within this context with fraction bars. These bars are visual aids for determining what fraction of the whole must be added or subtracted. Students then find the factor by which the whole should be multiplied to get the final increased or decreased dollar amount. For example, if an amount is increased by $\frac{1}{4}$, add $\frac{1}{4}$ to the whole to get the final dollar amount. The amount after the increase is $1\frac{1}{4}$ of the original amount and can be found by multiplying the original amount by $1\frac{1}{4}$, or $\frac{5}{4}$, or 1.25.

Planning

Students may work in small groups on problems 7–9. If necessary, discuss these problems in class.

Comments About the Solutions

8. This is a key problem. It requires rewriting the increase or decrease as a fraction.

9. This is a key problem too. Students may compute the profits in a variety of ways. Encourage students to show their strategies. Observe what strategies are used. This information could be useful when students encounter problems later on in this section.

Notes

10 This problem refers back to the strategy from Section B of using the percentage that remains.

12 In addition to converting the fractions to decimals and then multiplying, students may think of the fraction as a division; for example, write 3 ÷ 4 × 1257. Since calculators vary, ask students to test their calculators to see whether different calculators give the same results with the same keystrokes. If students have not yet completed the unit *Expressions and Formulas*, they may find the results surprising.

In problem 9, Ms. Jao calculated this year's profit for the bakery like this.

$$\frac{7}{10} \times 55{,}900 = 0.7 \times 55{,}900$$

She then used her calculator.

10. **a.** Compare Ms. Jao's calculation to the bakery profit calculation you made in problem 9. What is the same and what is different?

b. How would Ms. Jao calculate this year's profit for the Health and Beauty department, using multiplication with decimals?

Fractions can be written as decimals.

11. On **Student Activity Sheet 4**, connect the fraction and decimal that express the same number.

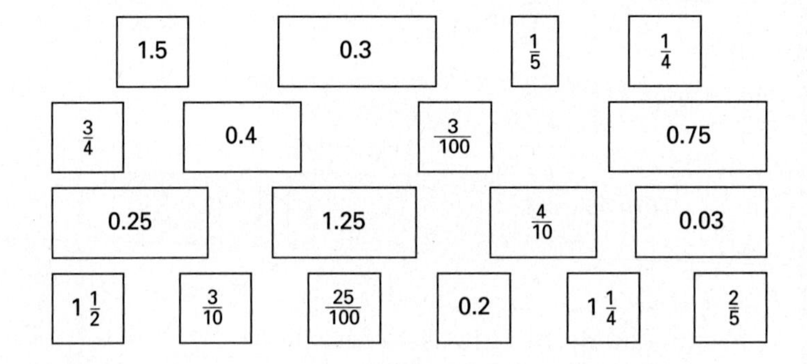

12. Describe how you can find the answer to these multiplication problems on a calculator that does not allow you to enter fractions.

a. $\frac{3}{4} \times 1{,}257$

b. $1\frac{1}{4} \times 1{,}257$

c. $\frac{17}{100} \times 1{,}257$

Reaching All Learners

Hands-On Learning

It may be helpful to have students cut apart the boxes from **Student Activity Sheet 4** and move the pieces around to make their matches for problem 11.

Intervention

Encourage students to connect a group of fractions and decimals that express the same number with lines of the same color.

Solutions and Samples

10. a. Answers will vary. Sample responses:

Some students may have calculated three tenths and subtracted this from $55,900.

Some may have used the same strategy as Ms. Jao's.

b. $\frac{3}{4} \times 46{,}800 = 0.75 \times 46{,}800$.

11.

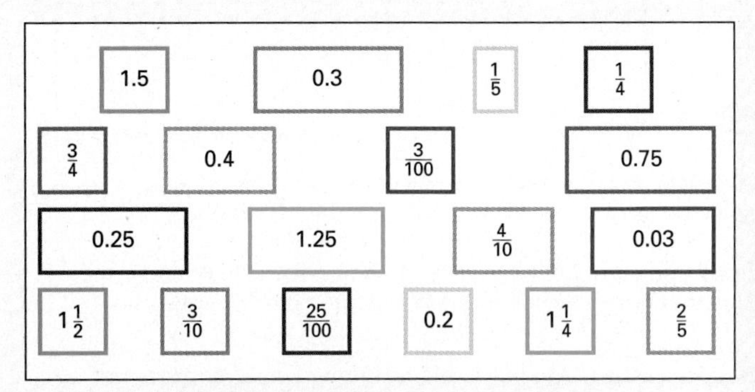

12. a. Responses may vary. Sample responses:

- $0.75 \times 1{,}257 =$
- $3 \div 4 \times 1{,}257 =$
- $1{,}257 \div 4 \times 3 =$

b. Responses may vary. Sample responses:

- $1.25 \times 1{,}257 =$
- $5 \div 4 \times 1{,}257 =$
- $1{,}257 + 1{,}257 \div 4 =$
- $1{,}257 \div 4 \times 5 =$

c. Responses may vary. Sample responses:

- $0.17 \times 1{,}257 =$
- $17 \div 100 \times 1{,}257 =$
- $1{,}257 \div 100 \times 17 =$

Hints and Comments

Materials

Student Activity Sheet 4 (one per student);
calculators (one per student);
colored pencils (optional);
scissors (optional)

Overview

Students review the relationship between fractions and decimals. They look for equivalent fractions and decimals. Then they describe how to use their calculators to solve multiplication problems that involve fractions.

About the Mathematics

The relationships between fractions, decimals, and percents are important to develop students' understanding of using a percent as an operator.

The underlying idea is that when students can use fractions and decimals as an operator, and they understand the relationship of percents and decimals, they will be able to understand how to use percents as an operator.

Planning

You may have students work individually on problems 10–12. Problem 11 can be assigned as homework. Discuss students' strategies for problem 12. You may make an inventory of all strategies that are used.

Many Changes

Notes

Ms. Jao decided to use percents to change the prices of some items in her store. She made this table.

Product	Old Price	Change	New Price	New Price as Percentage of Old Price
Whole Milk	$2.10	–10%		90%
Frozen Dinner	$4.68	–25%		
Roasted Turkey	$13.25	+25%		
6 Cans of Juice	$2.98	–5%		
Canned Salmon	$3.60	+15%		

13 Explain to students that "New Price as Percentage of Old Price" is a way of comparing the new price to the old price. The old price is 100%, and for a percent increase, the new price will be higher than 100%. For a percent decrease, the new price will be less than 100%.

13. Use **Student Activity Sheet 5** to fill in the columns labeled "New Price" and "New Price as Percentage of Old Price."

14 This problem summarizes the work to this point.

14. Describe and compare two ways of finding the sale price of cookies that normally sell for $4.98 but are now 15% off.

While Ms. Jao was working in her office, her two children, Jim and Michelle, came by to visit. She decided to take a break and have a glass of lemonade with them.

The children discussed the amount of lemonade in their glasses.

15 Discuss how to use the marked glasses as percent bars. Emphasize that percents are based on what we choose to be the whole or 100%.

15. **a.** Reflect Do you agree with Jim or Michelle? Defend your position.

b. Can the other person also be right? Why?

Assessment Pyramid

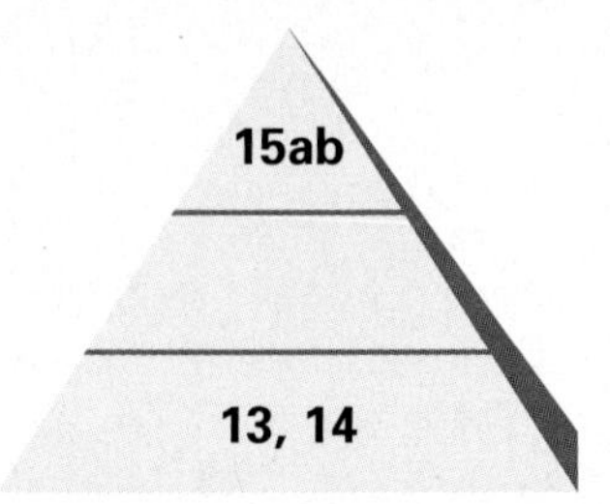

Understand common misconceptions of percent.

Calculate a percent of a number and sale price.

Reaching All Learners

Intervention

Asking students what number Jim is using as the whole and what number Michelle is using as the whole may help those who are unable to see that both can be correct.

Act It Out

Students can be assigned to take either Jim's or Michelle's side and argue why Jim or Michelle is correct. This may help struggling students see the dilemma.

Solutions and Samples

13.

Product	Old Price	Change	New Price	New Price as Percentage of Old Price
Whole Milk	\$2.10	-10%	\$1.89	90%
Frozen Dinner	\$4.68	-25%	\$3.51	75%
Roasted Turkey	\$13.25	+25%	\$16.56	125%
6 Cans of Juice	\$2.98	-5%	\$2.83	95%
Canned Salmon	\$3.60	+15%	\$4.14	115%

14. Strategies will vary. Sample strategies:

- Find 15% of \$4.98, which is \$0.75, and subtract that from \$4.98.

  \$4.98 – \$0.75 = \$4.23
- 100% – 15% = 85%

  Find 85% of \$4.98, which is 0.85 × \$4.98 = \$4.23.

15. a. Answers will vary, but both Jim and Michelle are correct.

Each glass is divided into five equal parts. Jim is correct if he considers the amount of lemonade in his glass to be 100%. The filled part of his glass is then divided into fourths. He can reason that the unfilled part of his glass is $\frac{1}{4}$ of the filled part, or 25%. Michelle can claim that since her glass is full and is divided into five equal parts, Jim has $\frac{1}{5}$ or 20% less than she does.

b. See the answer for problem 15a.

Hints and Comments

Materials

Student Activity Sheet 5 (one per student)
calculators (one per student)

Overview

Students describe changes in profit using percents and express the new price as a percent of the old price. Students compare percent increase and decrease problems.

About the Mathematics

At this point, two strategies have been developed for computing a change in price.

- The amount of increase or decrease is first computed and then added or subtracted from the original amount. For example, a 25% increase of \$12 is computed as 25% of \$12, which is \$3 and then \$12 + \$3 = \$15.
- The price change is computed by multiplying the percent of change by the original amount.

For example, a 25% increase of \$12 is computed as 125% (100% + 25%) of \$12, or 1.25 × \$12 or \$15.

Planning

Problem 14 may be used as Informal Assessment. Students may work in small groups on problem 15 to facilitate group discussions.

Comments About the Solutions

13. This is the same as problem 8, but here students use percents to describe the increase or decrease.

14. Students' strategies will show how they developed their number sense and their ability to use a percentage as an operator.

15. From Jim's point of view:

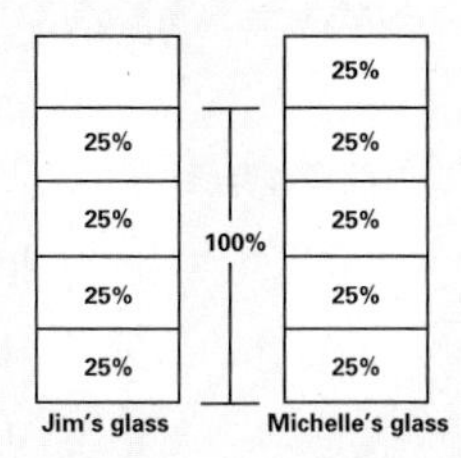

So Michelle has 25% more or 125% of what Jim has. From Michelle's point of view:

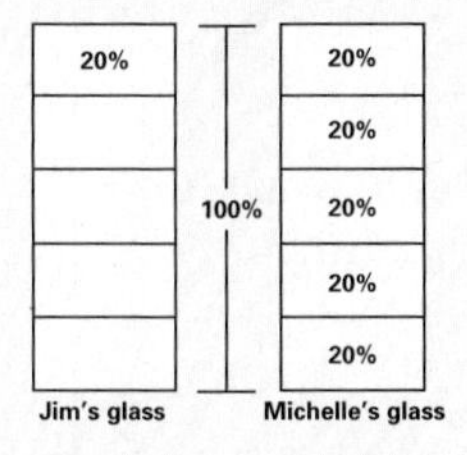

Notes

16 Students might want to try the situation with easier numbers so that they can see what is happening.

17 Encourage students to compare the amounts subtracted and added.

18 Encourage students to use arrow language to solve this problem.

After they finished their lemonade, Jim and Michelle went to Dale's Department Store to buy a birthday present for their friend Puno. Jim and Michelle agreed on a gift and took it to the cashier to make their purchase. The cashier made a mistake and gave them a 20% discount. When she caught her mistake, she decided to just add 20% of the total back on.

16. a. Do you think adding 20% of the total price corrects the mistake?

b. Copy and fill in the receipt.

Dale's Department Store

Nontaxable Merchandise	$23.70
–20%	$_____
TOTAL	$_____
+20%	$_____
TOTAL	$_____

17. Explain the effect of subtracting 20% of the price and then adding 20% of that total price back.

Dale reminded his employees to check the sale prices, using the percent discount and the sale price.

18. Find the original price of a T-shirt with a 20% discount and a sale price of $15.

Assessment Pyramid

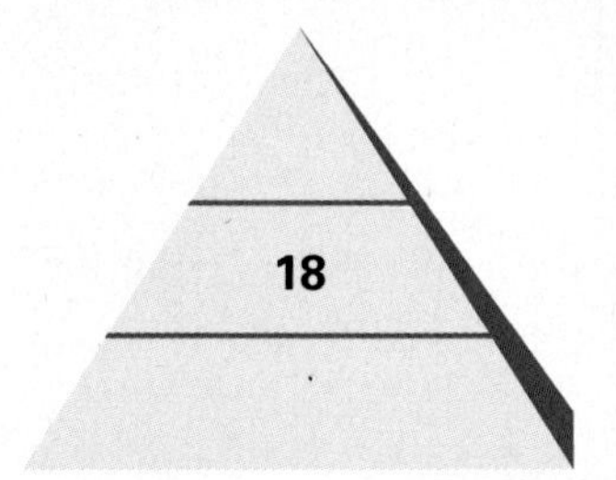

Find an original sale price using the sale price and discount.

Reaching All Learners

Intervention

Have students use whole dollar prices.

Visual Learners

A figure like the following, similar to the lemonade glasses, may be helpful for problem 17.

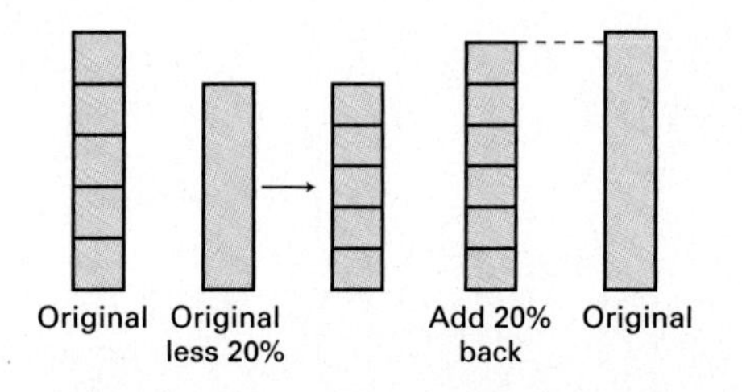

Original less 20%. Add 20% back on and it's a little smaller.

Solutions and Samples

16. a. No, it will not correct the mistake.

The cashier assumed that the 20% she deducted from the original price would be the same as adding 20% of the discounted price.

b.

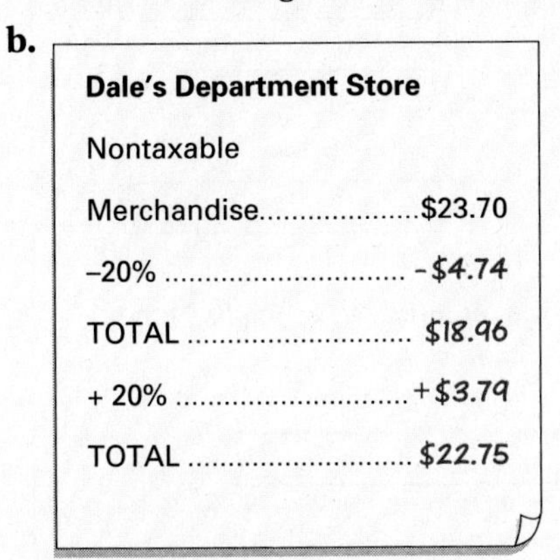

Dale's Department Store

Nontaxable

Merchandise.................... $23.70

–20% .... -$4.74

TOTAL $18.96

+ 20% .... +$3.79

TOTAL $22.75

17. Twenty percent of the original price is $4.74, and 20% of the discounted price is $3.79. So when the cashier tried to correct her mistake, she subtracted more ($4.74) than what she added ($3.79).

18. The original price is $18.75. Strategies will vary. Sample strategies:

- Using a bar:

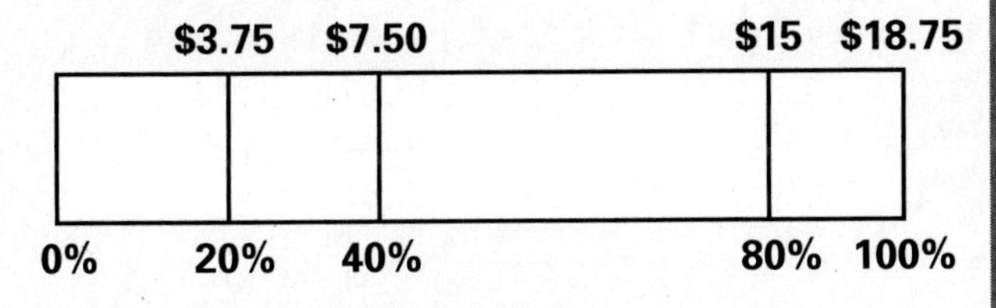

To get the price at 100% you can add $3.75 and $15, which is $18.75.

- $15 is 80% of the original price.

10% is $1.875 ($15 ÷ 8).

So 100% is 10 × $1.875 = $18.75.

Hints and Comments

Overview

Students solve and compare percent increase and decrease problems.

About the Mathematics

Problem 16 gives students experience avoiding the common mistake that 20% of the original amount is the same as 20% of the discounted amount. This can be explained by: Percents are determined by the base against which they are calculated.

This difference may be easier for students to see with a greater percent, such as 50%, and with visual support of a bar.

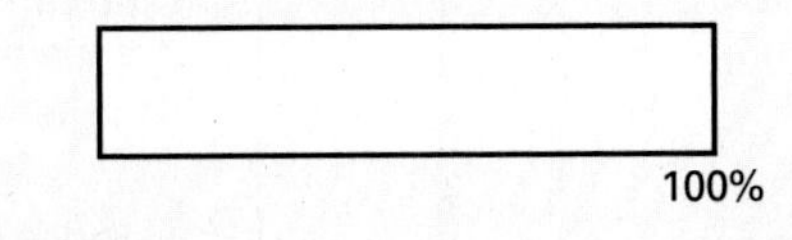

Add 50%.

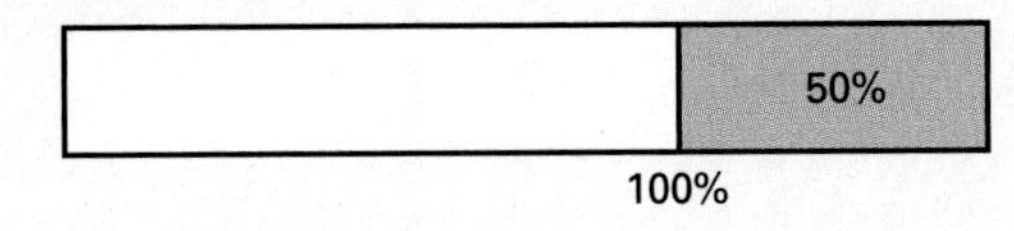

This bar now represents the total.

Now subtract 50% of the total.

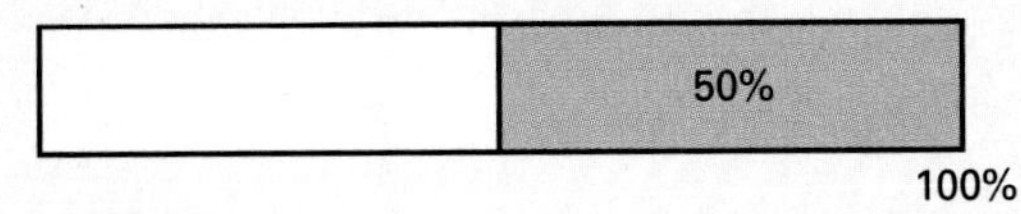

Planning

Have students work on problems 16–18 in small groups. Discuss students' strategies in class.

Comments About the Solutions

16. The lemonade glasses from problem 15 can be used to visually explain the structure of this problem. Take Jim's glass. Add 25% of the amount of lemonade, and then his glass is filled up. Now he has the same amount of lemonade as Michelle. You have to pour out 20% of Michelle's lemonade to get the original amount of lemonade of Jim's glass. Therefore, Jim has to pour out 20% of his lemonade to get his original amount of lemonade back.

17. Encourage students to compare the amounts subtracted and added.

18. Encourage students to use bars to solve this problem. It is important that they understand the structure of the problem: $15 is 80% of the original price.

Many Changes

Notes

The Summary on this page clearly shows the use of the bar model. At this point, students should be comfortable with the idea that you can calculate a discounted price by using the percent remaining. The bar model also shows a percent increase.

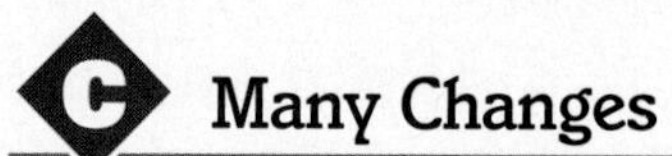

Many Changes

Summary

To calculate the sale price of an item with a discount given as a percent or fraction, you can do it with one multiplication calculation.

For example, suppose an item is discounted by 25%.

The discount is 25%, or $\frac{1}{4}$.

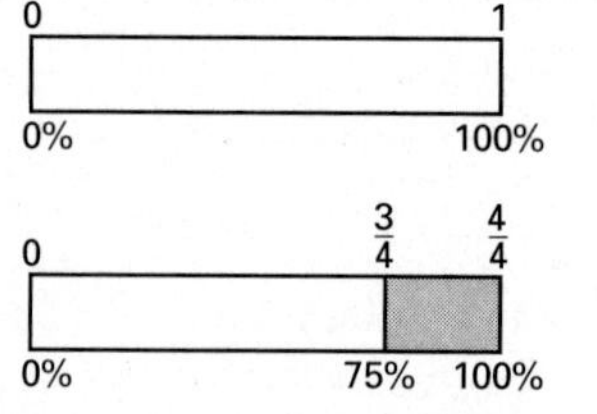

The new price is 75%, or, $\frac{3}{4}$, of the old price, so multiply $\frac{3}{4}$ times the original price.

Increasing a price by a percent is the same as taking 100% plus the percent increase of the price.

For example, increasing a price by 50% is the same as finding 150% of the price, or multiplying $1\frac{1}{2}$ times the original price.

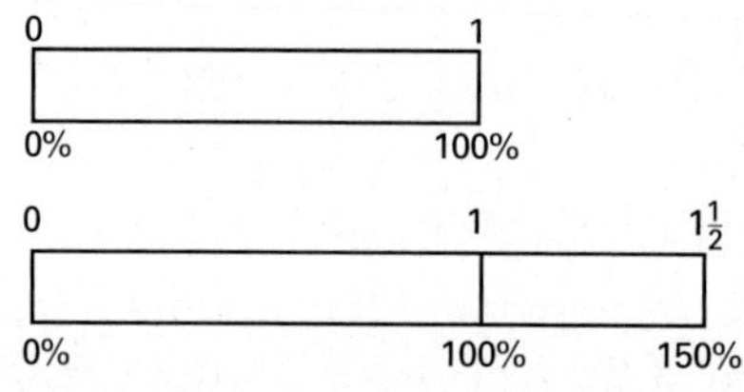

In other words, increasing by 50% is the same as multiplying the original price by $1\frac{1}{2}$ or 1.5.

Check Your Work

Save Supermarket orders fresh fruit each day. Tim records changes in weight on a chart. The manager compared today's weight to yesterday's weight on a chart.

Fruit Order	Change in Weight
Apples	One-quarter more
Pears	One-third less
Oranges	Two-fifths less
Bananas	Three-tenths more

1. Use bars to indicate the change in weight for each type of fruit Save Supermarket orders. Label the bars.

Assessment Pyramid

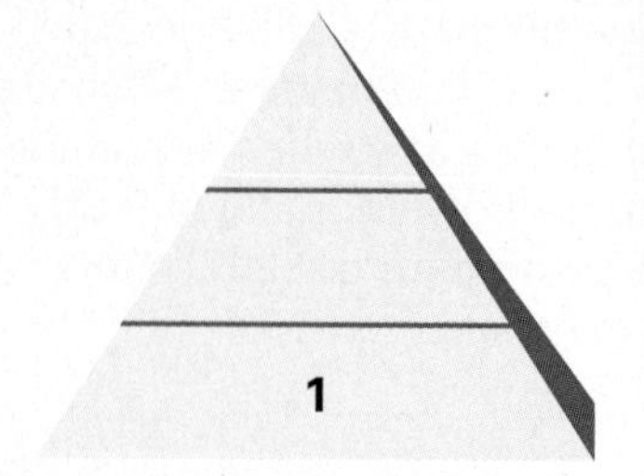

Assesses Section C Goals

Reaching All Learners

Parent Involvement

Students can be asked to use the Summary to explain to their parents what they have been learning. The Check Your Work questions then give the students a chance to demonstrate that understanding to their parents.

Solutions and Samples

Answers to Check Your Work

1. Answers will vary. Sample answers are shown.

Apples

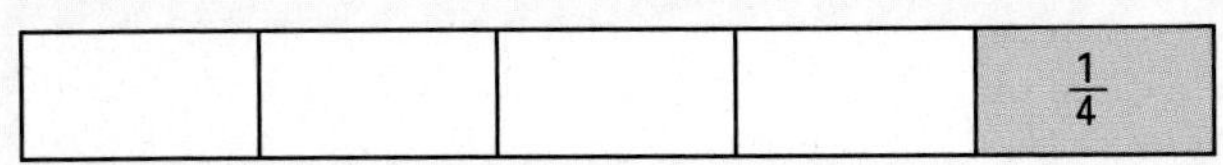

Pears

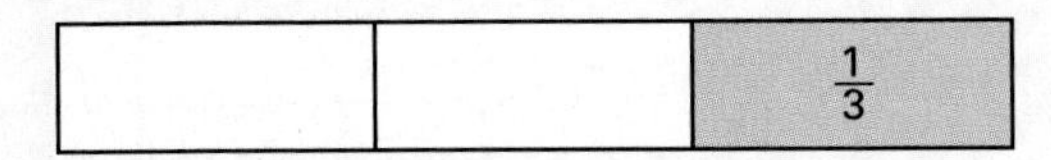

Oranges

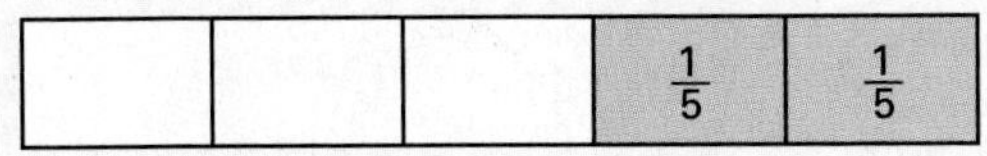

Bananas

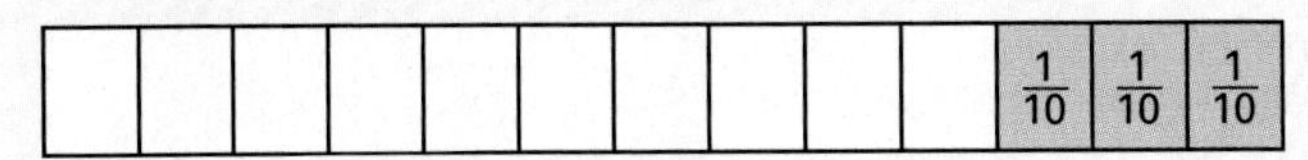

Hints and Comments

Overview

Students review the different strategies they have learned and used in this section.

Check Your Work

These problems are designed for student self-assessment. A student who can answer the questions correctly has understood enough of the concepts taught in the section to be able to start the next section. Students who have difficulties in answering the questions without help may need extra practice. This section is also useful for parents who want to help their children with their work.

Answers are provided in the Student Book. Have students discuss their answers with classmates.

Many Changes

Notes

The table below shows the weight of yesterday's fruit order.

Fruit Order	Weight Yesterday
Apples	80 kg
Pears	45 kg
Oranges	100 kg
Bananas	120 kg

2 Encourage students to justify their work using their bars from problem 1.

2. Use the information in both charts to find the weight of today's fruit order. Show your calculations.

3 Allow students to use various strategies to solve this problem. Some students may implicitly use the distributive property. Instead of calculating the discount for each item separately, they might find the discount on all the items by first adding the individual prices and then finding either 15% or 85%.

3. Tim buys an entire set of pots and pans at Dale's Department Store. Which discount saves him more money, $1.50 off each item or 15% off each item?

4. An item is discounted 20%. What fraction of the original price do you pay?

5. Describe how you can find the original price if you know the sale price is $42 and the original price was discounted 25%.

For Further Reflection

Consider an item that had an original price of $75.00. It was discounted 25%. Then it was discounted a second time, at 15% off the sale price. Is this the same as an original discount of 40%? Explain and show the calculations.

For Further Reflection

Students should be encouraged to draw a diagram to support their solution.

Assessment Pyramid

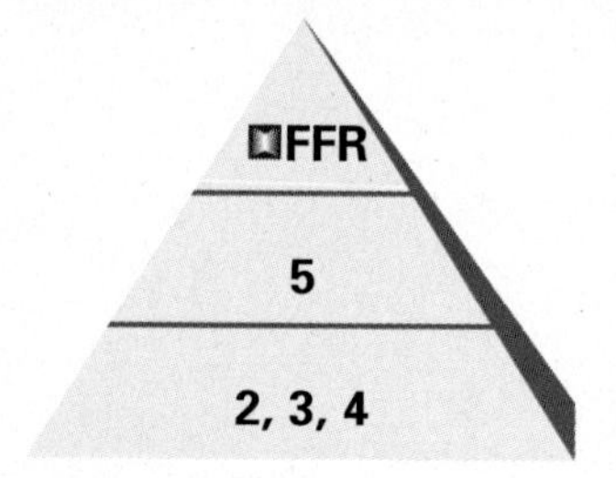

Assesses Section C goals

Reaching All Learners

Visual Learners

Problems 4 and 5 both lend themselves to bar model solution strategies.

Intervention

If students do not know how to get started, give the hint that they can try it for a price that they can choose by themselves. If it does not work for this price, then it is not true. If it works for this price, you still cannot be sure that it will work for any price.

Solutions and Samples

2. You may have used strategies like these.

Apples: $\frac{1}{4}$ more is 100 kg; $\frac{1}{4}$ of 80 kg is 20 kg; $\frac{1}{4}$ more is 100 kg (80 + 20).

Pears: $\frac{1}{3}$ less leaves 30 kg. $\frac{1}{3}$ of 45 is 15, and 45 − 15 is 30 kg.

Oranges: $\frac{2}{5}$ less is 60 kg. $\frac{1}{5}$ of 100 is 20 kg, so $\frac{3}{5}$ of 100 is 3 × 20 = 60 kg.

Bananas: $\frac{3}{10}$ more is 156 kg. $\frac{1}{10}$ of 120 kg is 12 kg, so $\frac{3}{10}$ of 120 is 3 × 12 = 36; 36 + 120 = 156 kg.

3. Tim saves more money with a discount of $1.50 for each item, which is a discount of $7.50 (5 × $1.50). Sample strategies:

- Calculating 15% of the total:

  15% of ($11.95 + $9.95 + $8.95 + 7.95 + 6.95)
  15% of $45.75 is a little more than $6.86, which is not as good as a $7.50 discount.

- Calculating 15% off each item using a calculator:

  0.15 × $11.95 + 0.15 x $9.95 + 0.15 × $8.95 + 0.15 × $7.95 + 0.15 × $6.95 = 6.8625 about $6.86, which is not as good as a $7.50 discount.

- Estimating 15% of total:

  Estimate of total is $46
  ($7 + $8 + $9 + $10 + $12).

  15% of $46, which is 10% + 5% of $46, which is $4.60 + $2.30 = $6.90, and this is less than the discount of $7.50.

  If you make a more accurate estimate:
  The total is $7 + $8 + $9 + $10 + $12 − 5 × $0.05 = $45.75.

  15% of $45.75 is about $6.86, which is less than $7.50.

4. You have to pay $\frac{4}{5}$ of the old price.

Sample strategy, using a percent bar:

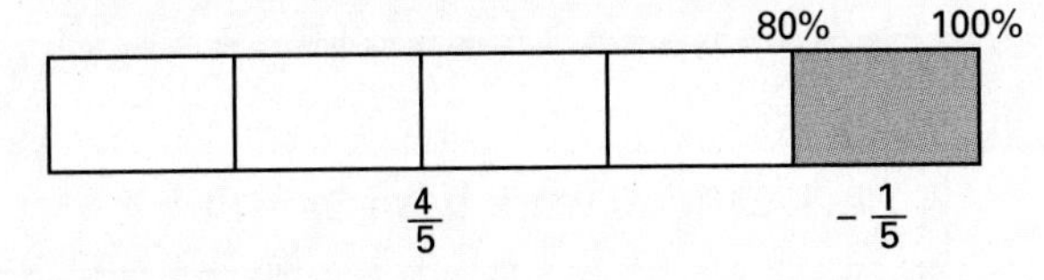

5. The original price is $56.

Note that the original price wasn't given here! There are several ways to solve this problem.

- Using a percent bar:

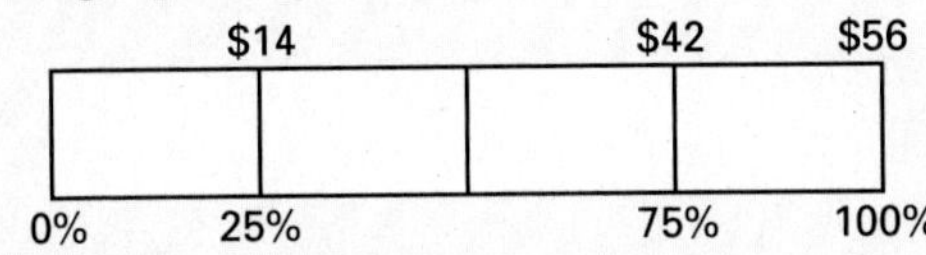

Since $42 is the sale price after a 25% discount, 75% or $\frac{3}{4}$ of the bar represents $42. So 25% of the bar is $14 and the whole bar has to be 4 of these, or $56.

Hints and Comments

Materials

calculators (one per student)

Planning

After students complete Section C, you may assign appropriate activities from the Additional Practice section, located on page 37 as homework.

- Using a double number line with fractions and decimals:

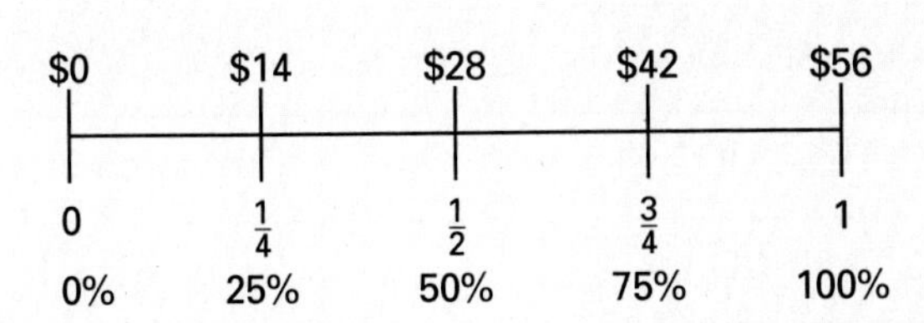

- Using a ratio table:

Price	$42	$14	$56
Percent	75%	25%	100%

For Further Reflection

No, it is not the same.

Explanations may vary. Sample explanation:

- Starting with an item priced at $20:

  A 25% discount is $\frac{1}{4}$ of $20, which is $5, so the discount price is $15.

  15% discount of $15 is $1.50 + $0.75, or $2.25. So the discount price is $15 − $2.25 = $12.75.

  A 40% discount of $20 is $8, so it is different.

Section Focus

Students investigate how percents are used to indicate reductions and enlargements of pictures on a photocopy machine. They use arrow language to describe the enlargements and reductions and to calculate the dimensions of the enlarged or reduced copy. Students further explore percents as operators in the context of discount, sales tax, and interest. The instructional focus of Section D is to:

- **solve percent increase and decrease problems involving measurements and**
- **calculate the money earned on interest from a savings account.**

Pacing and Planning

Day 12: Enlarge or Reduce		Student pages 27–28
INTRODUCTION	Problems 1–3	Calculate the length and width of a flyer.
CLASSWORK	Problems 4–7	Determine reduced measurements from a ratio table.
HOMEWORK	Problem 8	Find equivalent strategies for percent increase.

Day 13: Sales Tax		Student pages 28–30
INTRODUCTION	Problems 9 and 10	Find discount and sale price.
CLASSWORK	Problems 11–16	Calculate price, including tax, by multiplying.
HOMEWORK	Problems 17 and 18	Find the original price given a total price and the tax amount.

Day 14: Growing Interest		Student pages 31–34
INTRODUCTION	Review homework.	Review homework from Day 14.
CLASSWORK	Problems 19–21	Investigate compound interest.
HOMEWORK	Check Your Work and For Further Reflection	Students self-assess Section D goals

Additional Resources: Additional Practice, Section D, pages 37 and 38

Materials

Student Resources

No resources required.

Teachers Resources

No resources required.

Student Materials

Quantities listed are per pair of students, unless otherwise noted.

- Calculator (one per student)
- Centimeter ruler
- Brochures on savings plans from a local bank

* See Hints and Comments for optional materials.

Learning Lines

Concepts *Percents, Increase and Decrease*

Arrow strings as developed in the Algebra Strand are used to find the dimensions of enlarged or reduced photocopies and to connect the percent decrease and increase to multiplication. For example, the arrow string below describes a reduction to 80%.

Original length $\xrightarrow{\times 0.80}$ Reduced length

Concepts *Percents*

In this section, these arrow strings are used to further develop the concept of a percentage as operator. (For students the expression *one-multiplication* is used.)

For example, to calculate the final cost of an item with a 19% sales tax:

Price $\xrightarrow{\times 1.19}$ Total cost with tax

The concept of percents as operator is further investigated in the unit *Ratios and Rates.*

At the End of this Section: Learning Outcomes

Students can solve percent increase and decrease problems. They can choose a strategy they feel comfortable with: a ratio table, a percent bar, a one-multiplication, and/or the relationships between percents, fractions, and decimals. Students will have developed some understanding of the use of a percent as an operator.

Notes

This page sets the context for the beginning of the section. Be sure that students understand that copy machines can make enlargements and reductions, but resist having a discussion of the meaning of the percentages given. Students will grapple with this in problem 1.

More or Less

Enlarge or Reduce

Maritza, Laura, and Jamel are opening a new store called Roll On. To advertise the grand opening, Maritza and Jamel designed a flyer with a picture of an in-line skater.

Here is the picture that Maritza and Jamel want to use for the flyer.

They realized that the picture had to be reduced to fit on the flyer. Laura suggested that they use a photocopier to see what the reduced picture would look like. Jamel and Maritza agreed. They found a photocopier that could reduce originals to 25 percent and enlarge originals to 400 percent.

Reaching All Learners

English Language Learners

Be sure students understand what a flyer is since this is the context for the first problems.

Hints and Comments

Overview

Students apply and extend their knowledge of percent decrease and increase as they investigate a problem context involving the reduction and enlargement of flyers.

About the Mathematics

In this section, making reductions and enlargements using a photocopier helps to develop the concept of percents as operators.

Planning

Begin this section by asking students about their experiences using copy machines. Focus the discussion on machines that can reduce and enlarge. Some students may know that these machines use percents to indicate how much they enlarge or reduce. Show students that a 75% reduction produces a copy whose dimensions are 75% of the dimensions of the original.

More or Less

Notes

2a Have students assume that the original dimensions are 10 cm × 15 cm.

3 Students should not be surprised that the result of two 50% reductions is not a 100% reduction. Once students get their result in part **c**, ask why this number makes sense.

3bc Encourage students to use arrow language.

4 Remind students to use ratio table strategies. Let them know that they do not have to complete the table in the order presented.

1. **Reflect** What does it mean to reduce to 25 percent and enlarge to 400 percent? Give examples to illustrate your explanation.

2. a. Suppose they reduce the picture to 50%. What will the new width and length be? Show your calculations.

   b. Complete the arrow string to describe a reduction to 50%.

original length $\xrightarrow{\times \ldots}$ reduced length

The result of this reduction is still too large to fit on the flyer.

Maritza suggests, "Just take the reduced copy and reduce it again to 50%. Then we will see if that fits."

3. a. What are the width and length after two successive reductions to 50%?

   b. Describe the calculation to make two reductions of 50%.

   c. How can they get the same result, starting with the original and using just one reduction?

The group has gone to a lot of trouble to find the effect of a reduction. It would be a lot easier if the print shop had a chart that shows the measurements of an object after it is reduced.

4. Copy and fill in the table below for making a reduction to 30%.

Original Length (in cm)	10	15	20	1	2	3	4	5
Length Reduced to 30%								

5. a. How can you use a calculator to find the effect of a reduction to 30%?

   b. Use arrow language to describe this calculation.

Assessment Pyramid

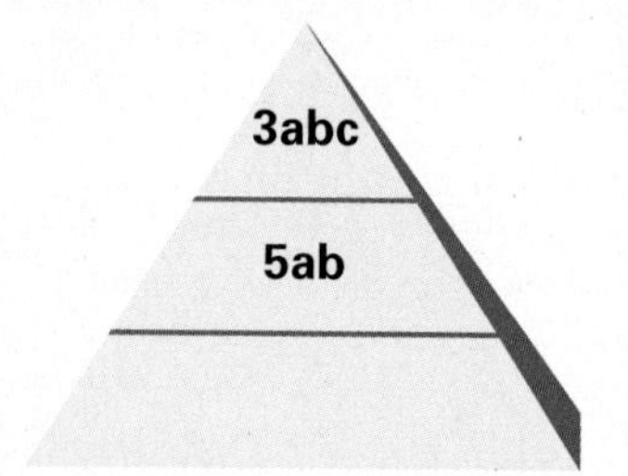

Understand multiplicative decrease.

Use percents as operators.

Reaching All Learners

Intervention

In problem 2, be sure that students write either $\frac{1}{2}$ or 0.5. Some students have a tendency to write 2, thinking about dividing by two.

Accommodation

You can copy the ratio table from problem 4 so that students do not have to spend time drawing the table.

Solutions and Samples

1. Answers will vary. Sample response:

- When a picture is reduced to 25%, the dimensions of the sides are $\frac{1}{4}$ of the original dimensions.

When a picture is enlarged to 400%, the dimensions of the sides are 4 × the original dimensions.

- If a picture measures 16 cm by 20 cm, it will be reduced to 4 cm by 5 cm. (25% of 16 cm is 4 cm and 25% of 20 cm is 5 cm).

If a picture measures 2 cm by 3 cm, it will be enlarged to 8 cm by 12 cm (400% is four times).

2. a. This answer assumes that the picture dimensions are 10 cm by 15 cm. Width = 5 cm, length = 7.5 cm.

b. original length $\xrightarrow{\times \frac{1}{2}}$ reduced length

3. a. Width = 2.5 cm, length = 3.75 cm.

b. Answers may vary.

- divide by 2 and then divide by 2 again
- half and then half again
- divide by 4
- multiply by 0.25 (half of half is one-fourth which is 0.25)
- original length $\xrightarrow{\times \frac{1}{2}}$ ___ $\xrightarrow{\times \frac{1}{2}}$ reduced length

c. By reducing to 25%

4.

Original Length (in cm)	10	15	20	1	2	3	4	5
Length Reduced to 30%	3	4.5	6	0.3	0.6	0.9	1.2	1.5

5. a. Multiply the original length and width by 0.3.

b. original length $\xrightarrow{\times 0.3}$ reduced length

Hints and Comments

Materials

centimeter ruler (one per pair of students)

Overview

Students explain what a photocopy machine actually does when it reduces a picture to 25% and enlarges it to 400% of the original size. Students use arrow language to describe reductions. They use arrow language and a calculator to find the dimensions of both first and second reductions.

About the Mathematics

The use of arrow language will further develop the idea of percents as an operator. Students may remember from the unit *Expressions and Formulas* how to work with arrow language.

Some students may confuse size with dimensions. When the picture is reduced to 80%, for example, the dimensions are reduced to 80%. The area (or size), however, is reduced to 64% of the original.

The concepts of reduction, enlargement, ratio, and scale changes will be revisited in the unit *Ratios and Rates.*

Planning

Students may work in small groups on problems 1–5. A class discussion should emphasize students' solutions and strategies for problems 3b and 4.

Comments About the Solutions

1. You may want to make a distinction between "reducing by 80%" and "reducing to 80%." For example, a picture 10 cm by 10 cm reduced "to" 80% means the length and width are each reduced by 20%, or they are 80% of their original length. The picture becomes 8 cm by 8 cm.

When the 10 cm by 10 cm picture is reduced "by" 80%, it means that the dimensions are reduced by 80% (or reduced to 20%), and the length of each side will become 2 cm.

Extension

Problem 3 provides an opportunity to discuss the relationship between the length and area of the original picture and the length and area of the reduced picture. Some students may notice that the reduced picture has dimensions half of the original picture, but it fits four times on the original picture. Therefore, the area is $\frac{1}{4}$ of the area of the original picture.

More or Less

Notes

8 This problem is difficult. Part **a** asks students if they think it is possible and why they think that without their having to prove it. Part **b** asks for the numbers to make it work.

9 This should be a review of the previous section for students. Make sure students are clear that Maritza is calculating the discount, not the sale price.

The group wants to make a poster using the original picture. This time the picture has to be enlarged.

6. Find the dimensions of a picture 10 centimeters (cm) by 15 cm enlarged to 200%. Show your calculations.

The result is too small for the poster, so they decide to enlarge the original picture to 250%.

7. a. Find the dimensions of the picture (10 cm by 15 cm) enlarged to 250%. Show your calculations.

b. Use arrow language to describe this calculation.

Suppose you want to make an enlargement to 200%. The photocopier you are using enlarges to only 150%.

8. a. Will two enlargements to 150% give the desired result? Explain.

b. Find two enlargements that can be used with this photocopier to produce a final enlargement as close as possible to 200%. Copy the arrow string to describe your result.

original length $\xrightarrow{\times \ldots}$ ……. $\xrightarrow{\times \ldots}$ enlarged length

Discount

Maritza and Jamel went to the Office Supply Store to buy a frame for the poster. There were several frames for sale. Maritza liked the one shown on the left.

9. a. What is the discount in dollars?

b. Maritza calculated the discount with one multiplication: $0.25 \times \$12.80$.

Explain why this is correct. The percent bar can be helpful for finding an explanation.

$0 — $12.80 | discount 25% | 0% — 100%

c. Calculate the sale price for this frame.

Assessment Pyramid

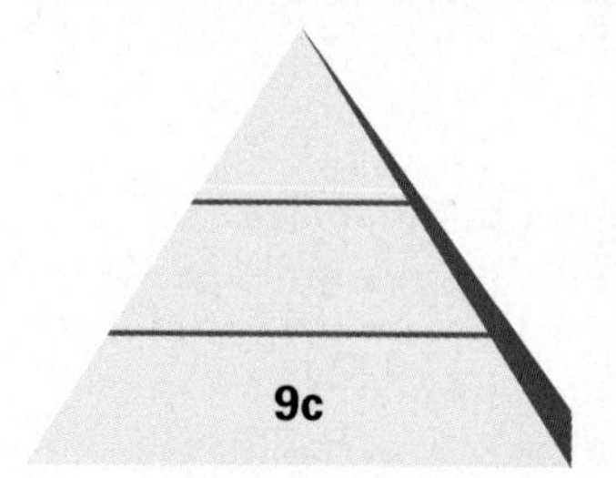

Calculate sale and discount price.

Reaching All Learners

Extension

Students could be challenged in problem 7 to figure out how to set the machine if they were going to use the 200% enlargement to get the 250% enlargement.

Intervention

For students who are having difficulty with problem 8b, ask, *What has to be true about the two numbers you are looking for?* (The product of the numbers must be two.)

Solutions and Samples

6. The dimensions are 20 cm by 30 cm.
Sample calculation:
$10 \times 2 = 20$ cm and $15 \times 2 = 30$ cm.

7. a. The dimensions are 25 cm by 37.5 cm.
Sample calculation:
$10 \times 2.5 = 25$ cm and
$15 \times 2.5 = 37.5$ cm.

b. original length $\xrightarrow{\times 2.50}$ enlarged length

8. a. No.

Sample explanations:

- original length $\xrightarrow{\times 1.5}$ ___ $\xrightarrow{\times 1.5}$ enlarged length is the same as original length $\xrightarrow{\times 2.25}$ enlarged length
- If I have a picture with dimensions of 4 cm by 4 cm and I enlarge it 150%, then the new dimensions are 6 cm by 6 cm. If I enlarge this to 150%, then the new dimensions are 9 cm by 9 cm, and this is more than two times the original dimensions.
- If you calculate *number* × 1.5 ×1.5, then it is the same as *number* × 2.25, and this is more than × 2.

b. Answers may vary.

Sample answers:

- Two enlargements to 140%, gives

original length $\xrightarrow{\times 1.4}$ ___ $\xrightarrow{\times 1.4}$ enlarged length, or original length $\xrightarrow{\times 1.96}$ enlarged length ($1.4 \times 1.4 = 1.96$)

- I first used an enlargement of 150%. Now I have to find a number so that $1.5 \times ? = 2$

I calculated $2 \div 1.5$ which is 1.33, so the second enlargement is 133%.

9. a. $3.20

b. 25% of something is the same as $\frac{1}{4}$ part, or times $\frac{1}{4}$, and this is same as times 0.25.

c. The sales price is $9.60.

Hints and Comments

Materials
calculators (one per student)

Overview

Students calculate the dimensions of the picture enlarged to 200% and to 250%. They also use arrow language to describe the 250% enlargement. They find a first and second enlargement that will have the same result as one enlargement of 200%.

Students reinforce their understanding of the use of a percent as operator in the context of discount.

About the Mathematics

Students may remember from the unit *Expressions and Formulas* how two arrows can be shortened to one arrow. (Refer to the solutions to problem 8 in the solution column.)

Planning

You may have students work in small groups on problems 6-8. Problem 9 can be assigned as homework or used as Informal Assessment.

Comments About the Solutions

8. Since there are no picture dimensions given, some students may not know how to solve this problem. You may give the hint that they are allowed to use a picture with dimensions they make up by themselves, for example 4 cm by 4 cm.

8. b. The two enlargements do not have to be the same percentage.

An accurate answer can be found by using the square root of 2, which gives two enlargements of 141%.

Students can use a strategy of trial and error, but they can also try to develop a more straightforward strategy.

9. Students' explanations will show how they developed their number sense and their ability of using a percentage as an operator.

Extension

Ask students, *How would you enlarge a picture to 150% using a photocopy machine that only enlarges to 120%?* Students will notice that you have to enlarge it more then two times.

Possible solutions:
114%, 114%, 114% results in 148% of the original;
120%, 120%, 104% results in almost 150%.

Notes

11 This calculation strategy was hinted at in Section C. In that problem, the bar graph gave visual support. At this point students should be clear about why the calculation makes sense. You may encourage students to use a percent bar in their explanations.

12a Students should be able to easily calculate 8% of $100. Then each successive column is a division by 10.

Ask students what they notice when they have filled in the dollar amounts in the table. Can they explain this?

12b Have students share their strategies for this problem.

10. a. Explain one multiplication that can be used to calculate the discount of this frame.

b. Find the sale price of this frame.

Maritza and Jamel decided to buy this frame. When they checked out, they saw the cashier use a calculator to calculate the sale price.

15 ☒ 0.65 ⊟

11. Reflect Explain why this method works for calculating the sale price.

Sales Tax

Maritza and Jamel paid more than $9.75 for the frame. When they looked at the bill, they noticed a **sales tax** added to their purchase. Sales taxes help pay for local community services.

In many cities, the sales tax is 8%. So for an item priced at $20, you pay $20 plus 8% of $20.

Here are three ways to calculate the sales tax (8%) for a $20 purchase.

- One method uses a **ratio table.**

12. a. Copy the ratio table and fill in the dollar amounts for an 8% tax.

Price (in dollars)	$100	$10	$1	$0.10	
8% Tax (in dollars)					

b. Use this ratio table to find the sales tax (8%) for a $20 purchase.

- Another method uses a **percent bar.**

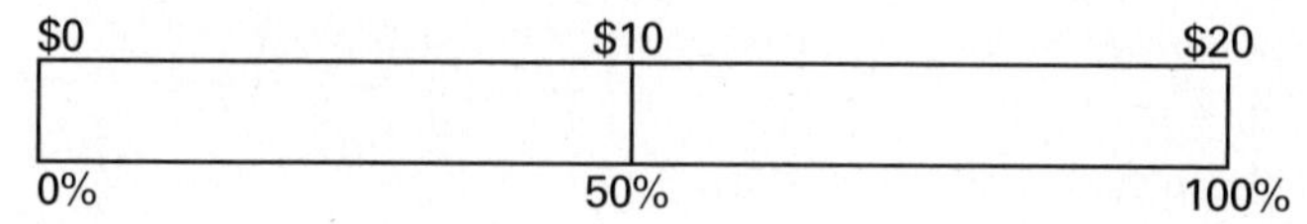

13. Copy this percent bar in your notebook and use it to find the sales tax (8%) for a $20 purchase.

Assessment Pyramid

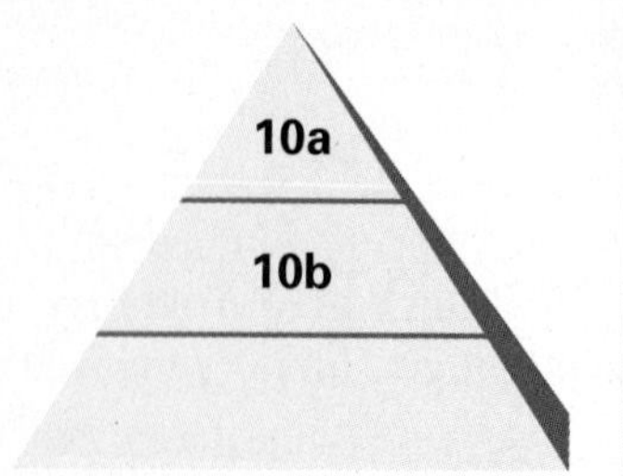

Explore use of percents as operators.

Calculate discount and sale price.

Reaching All Learners

Vocabulary Building

Review the terms *sales tax, amount paid,* and *marked price.* The rate of sales tax varies based on the state and municipality. Tax rate information can be found at http://www.taxadmin.org/fta/rate/sl_sales.html.

Solutions and Samples

10. a. To calculate the discount you can use

$15 × 0.35

b. The sale price is $9.75.

Sample strategy:

Students may use their answer from **a** to calculate the discount amount ($5.25) and subtract this from the original price ($15 – $5.25 = $9.75).

11. Explanations may vary. Sample explanation: The discount is 35%, so you pay 65%.

35% discount

100%

65% of $15 can be calculated by 0.65 × $15, or $15 × 0.65.

12. a. and **b.**

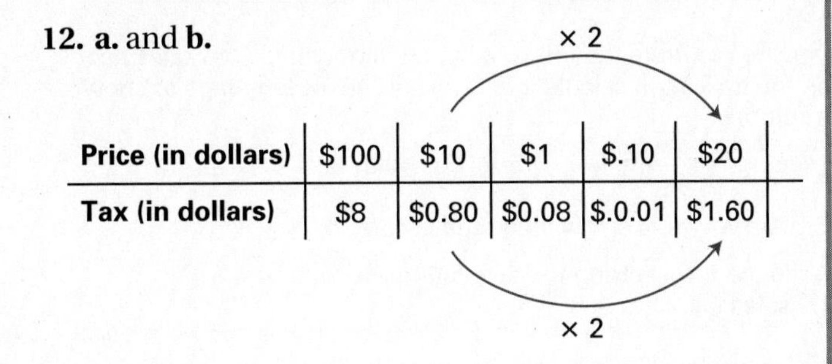

Price (in dollars)	$100	$10	$1	$.10	$20
Tax (in dollars)	$8	$0.80	$0.08	$.0.01	$1.60

13.

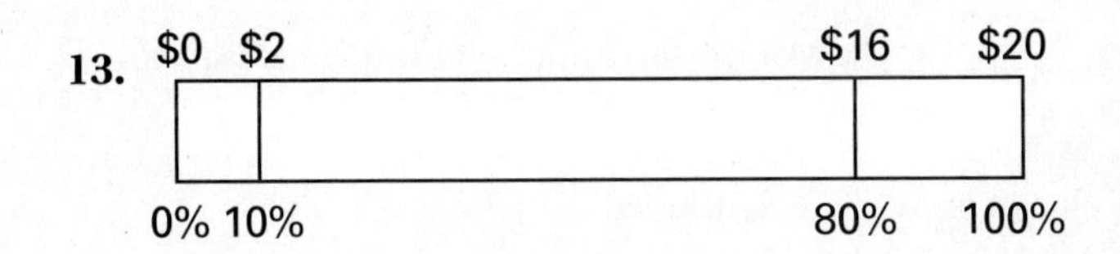

80% of $20 is $16, so 8% of $20 is $1.60.

Hints and Comments

Materials

calculators (one per student)

Overview

Students explain how a one multiplication can be used to find the discount amount and the sale price when the discount is 15%. On this page and the page that follows, students explore different methods to find the sales tax of items: using a ratio table, a percent bar, and arrow language.

About the Mathematics

The two strategies to calculate the sale price after a given percentage discount is revisited are:

- The amount of decrease is first computed and then subtracted from the original amount.
- The price change is computed by multiplying the percent of change by the original amount.

The amounts in the ratio table (problem 12) may focus on the ratio aspect of percentages: a tax of 8% is the same as eight dollars out of hundred dollars, or eight cents for every dollar (100 cents).

Planning

You may have students work individually on problems 10 and 11. These problems can be used as informal assessment. You may discuss problems 11 and 12 in class.

Notes

14 Students should be encouraged to make more divisions on the percent bar to find 8%.

16 In the class discussion, you may ask students to compare the arrow string that can be used to calculate the tax and the arrow string that can be used to find the total cost with tax. Ask, *How can you see from an arrow string whether or not the tax is included?*

- A third method uses **arrow language**.

  Price $\xrightarrow{\times\ldots}$ Tax amount

  It helps to remember the benchmark relationships for 1%, which are $\frac{1}{100}$ and 0.01.

14. a. What fraction corresponds to 8%?

b. What decimal corresponds to 8%?

c. Use arrow language (and a calculator) to show how to find the sales tax (8%) for a $20 purchase.

15. Copy the chart and fill in the last two rows. Use a sales tax of 19%.

Price in Dollars	$100.00	$10.00	$1.00
Tax in Dollars			
Total Cost with Tax			

Laura wants to compute the final cost of an item with a 19% sales tax, using one multiplication calculation. She uses arrow language to show what to multiply.

Price $\xrightarrow{\times 1.19}$ Total cost with tax

16. a. Explain why this arrow language is correct.

b. Write the arrow string for calculating the total cost with an 8% sales tax.

As Maritza and Jamel left Save Supermarket, Jamel bought the items on the left.

17. Find Jamel's total bill, with a sales tax of 8% included.

Maritza paid $12.63 at Save Supermarket. She wonders how much of the dollar amount is tax. The sales tax is 8%.

18. a. How can Maritza find out using arrow language?

b. Calculate the tax Maritza paid.

Assessment Pyramid

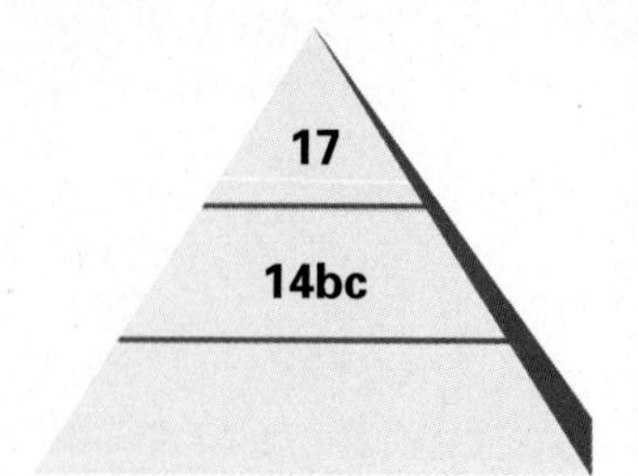

Use percents as operators. Relate percents to fractions and decimals.

Reaching All Learners

Advanced Learners

After problem 16, students could be asked how calculating the price with sales tax in one step is like calculating a sale price in one step.

Solutions and Samples

14. a. $\frac{8}{100}$

b. 0.08

c. $\$20 \xrightarrow{\times 0.08} \$1.60$

15.

Price (in dollars)	$100.00	$10.00	$1.00
Tax (in dollars)	$19.00	$1.90	$0.19
Total Cost with Tax	$119.00	$11.90	$1.19

16. a. Explanations may vary.

Sample explanation:

- 19% added means that you have 100% and 19%, which together is 119%, so you have to do × 1.19.
- using the table from problem 15: In the last column you see that for each dollar, you have to pay $1.19, so you have to multiply the price by 1.19.
- Some students may use a bar chart and add percents to explain why the formula is correct.

$0

100% Original Price	19% Tax

0% 100% 119%

The bar shows that the price including tax is 100% + 19% = 119%.

b. Price $\xrightarrow{\times 1.08}$ Total cost with tax

17.

Paper towels	$0.88
Peanuts	$1.90
Chicken	$4.98
Dish soap	$2.33
Apples	$0.92
Total	$11.01

Students may have made different calculations for the total price with sales tax.

Sample calculations:

- $11.01 × 1.08 = $11.89
- $11.01 + 0.08 × $11.01 = $11.01 + $0.88 = $11.89

18. a. Different responses are possible.

Sample response:

She can make an arrow string:

Original price $\xrightarrow{\times 1.08}$ $12.63

and then figure out what the original price is by calculating backwards.

Hints and Comments

Materials

calculators (one per student)

Overview

Students use a percent bar to find the sales tax. They make connections between percents, fractions, and decimals to find the sales tax. Students use arrow language to find the tax and to find the total cost with tax.

About the Mathematics

This bar chart shows that an 8% tax is added on to the original price to illustrate the total cost to the customer.

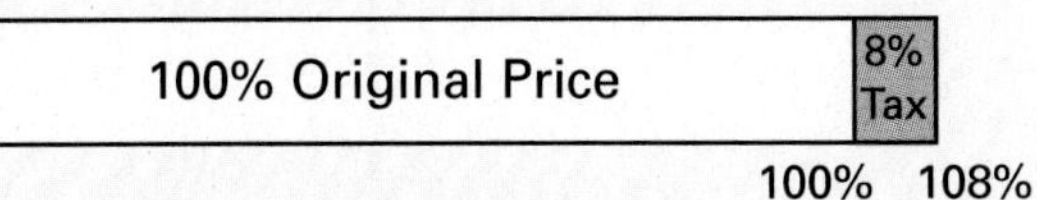

To calculate the total cost after tax, which is 108% of the original price, multiply the original price by 1.08. Arrow language can be used to calculate the price with 8% sales tax.

original price $\xrightarrow{\times 1.08}$ price with tax

Reverse arrow strings can be used in problem 18 to determine the original price.

Original price $\xrightarrow{\times 1.08}$ Price with tax

Original price $\xleftarrow{\div 1.08}$ Price with tax

See more Hints and Comments on page 63.

b. Different strategies are possible.

- Using a reverse arrow string:

  Original price $\xleftarrow{\times 1.08}$ $12.63

  $12.63 ÷ 1.08 = $11.69 is the original price, so the tax is $12.63 − $11.69 = $0.94.

- Using a percent bar:

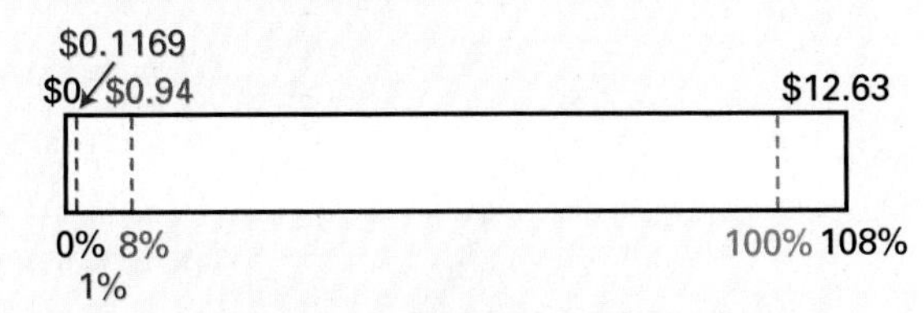

- Using a ratio table:

Price (in dollars)	$12.63	$0.1169	$0.94
Tax (in dollars)	108%	1%	8%

÷ 108 × 8

Notes

20a Encourage students to add 2% to 100% and then use this percentage to create an arrow string. This solution strategy will be useful when they solve problems **b** and **c**.

21 It is important that students see that after the first of each year, they are earning interest on the interest that was paid the previous year. This is called *compound interest.*

Growing Interest

Laura visited the local bank to open business accounts for their new store, Roll On. She spoke with Leticia Beligrado. When she finished setting up the accounts, she asked Ms. Beligrado to make a donation for the grand opening. Ms. Beligrado was willing to donate a $250 savings account as a grand opening prize, but she wanted to make the prize more attractive by specifying that the money must stay in the bank for three years. The savings account earns 2% **interest** every year.

19. **Reflect** Research the savings plans available at your local bank. Write a paragraph describing the options.

If you win the grand opening prize, you would begin with $250 in the savings account. With a 2% annual interest rate, the bank would add 2% of $250 by the end of the first year. As a result, you would have 102% of the original prize.

0% 100% 102%

20. a. How much money would you have after one year?
    b. The savings account would earn an additional 2% of the new balance by the end of the next year. How much money would be in your account at the end of the second year?
    c. At the end of the third year?

The money in the account grows quite nicely in just a few years.

21. **Reflect** Explain why the total interest earned grows larger each year.

Assessment Pyramid

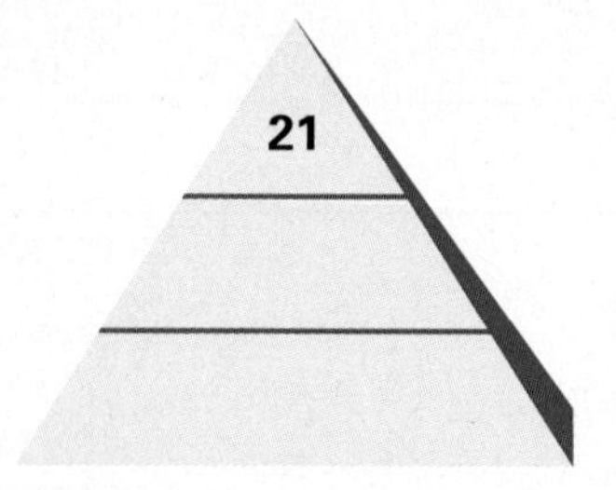

Explore multiplicative increase and decrease.

Reaching All Learners

Vocabulary Building

Interest is the money paid on an account in a bank. It is expressed as a percent.

Extension

Have students make up an original amount and a certain percent annual interest rate and find the number of years it takes for the money to double.

Solutions and Samples

19. Answers will vary.

20. a. Answer: $255

Students may either use one multiplication $250 × 1.02, or calculate first 2% of $250 and add this to $250.

b. $260.10

c. $265.30

21. Answers will vary. Sample response:

The interest earned is based on the amount of money you have in the savings account. If you have more money in the savings account each year, then you will earn more interest.

Hints and Comments

Materials

brochures on savings plans from a local bank (one per group);
calculators (one per student)

Overview

Students solve two more tax problems.
Then they continue using percents in the context of savings accounts and interest rates.

About the Mathematics

Problems 19–20 are an introduction to exponential growth, a subject that will be further elaborated in the unit *Ups and Downs.*

Planning

Students can work in small groups on problems 19–21.
Discuss students' answers and strategies for problem 20.

Comments About the Solutions

19. If students have not had personal experience with savings and loans or other banking institutions, this exercise will help them become familiar with them and the programs they offer.

20. b. For most students, this problem will be a first exposure to compound interest.

20. c. You can expect many interesting comments from students. This problem again emphasizes the relative nature of percents and the fact that the amount of interest earned each year depends on the amount of money in the account.

More or Less

Notes

The Summary reviews each of the techniques used in the section for calculating percent increase and decrease. It is important that students realize that sales tax and interest are both percent increases.

More or Less

In this section, you studied **percent increase** and **decrease** and applied it to resizing pictures and calculating **sales tax** and **interest**.

There are many tools you can use to calculate a percent increase or decrease.

- Use a **ratio table**.

For a percent increase, to find the tax and total cost using a sales tax of 8%:

Price in Dollars	$100	$10	$1	$12
Tax in Dollars	$8	$0.80	$0.08	$0.96
Total Cost	$108	$10.80	$1.08	$12.96

- Use a **percent bar**.

For a percent decrease, to find the sale price of a $12.80 item with a 25% discount:

$0 $9.60 $12.80
discount 25%
0% 75% 100%

For a percent increase, to find this year's profit increased 25% from last year's profit of $12,800:

$0 $12,800 $16,000
increase 25%
0% 100% 125%

Reaching All Learners

Parent Involvement

Students should go over the Summary with their parents so that they can show their parents the strategies they have learned.

Hints and Comments

Overview

Students read the Summary, that is continued on the next page and that reviews the main methods used to determine percent increases and decreases in this section.

Notes

2 Students may try various reductions, hoping to hit the correct dimensions. Encourage the use of a more systematic strategy like a ratio table, bar, or arrow language.

- Use a **double number line.**

For a percent decrease, to find the length of a 20-cm photo reduced to 80%:

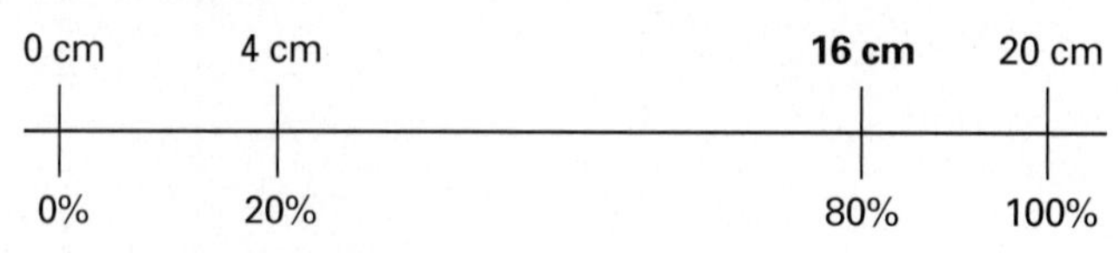

- Use **arrow language.**

For a percent increase, to find the total cost of an item with a 19% sales tax included:

Price $\xrightarrow{\times 1.19}$ Total, tax included

Check Your Work

Brenda and Kim are writing an article for the school newspaper. They need to reduce a photo with dimensions 12 cm by 18 cm.

1. a. What are the new dimensions of the picture if it is reduced to 50%?

b. If the original picture is reduced to 75%?

Afterward, the layout editor informs them that she allotted a blank space of 5 cm by 10 cm for their photo.

2. What reduction can Brenda and Kim use to fit their photo in the allotted blank space?

Ron and Ben are designing a poster for the school band concert. They have a picture they want to make 5 times as long and wide as it is now.

3. a. What enlargement would they have to make to have all measurements 5 times as big?

Assessment Pyramid

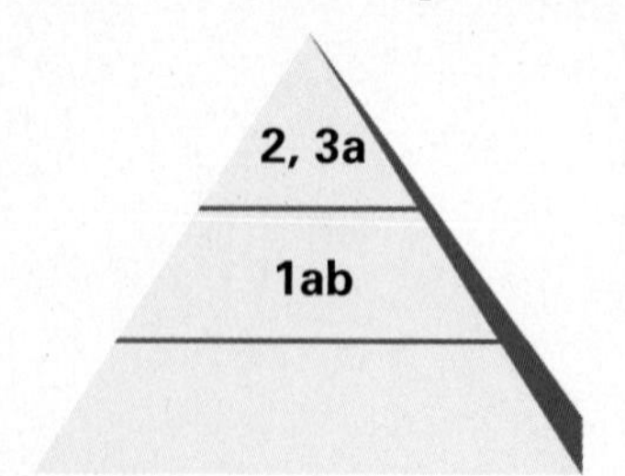

Assesses Section D Goals

Reaching All Learners

Extension

You may want to ask students to share the similarities and differences they noticed between the ratio table, double number line, and percent bar.

Solutions and Samples

Answers to Check Your Work

1. a. The new measurements are 6 cm by 9 cm.
   Sample calculations:

   50% of 12 cm is $\frac{1}{2}$ of 12 cm or 6 cm.

   50% of 18 cm is half of 18 cm or 9 cm.

   b. The new measurements are 9 cm by 13.5 cm.
   Sample calculations:

   Reduced to 75%, new measurements are $\frac{3}{4}$ of old measurements.

   $\frac{1}{4}$ of 12 cm is 3 cm, and $\frac{3}{4}$ is 3 times as much, so 3×3 cm = 9 cm.

   $\frac{1}{4}$ of 18 cm is $18 \div 4 = 4.5$ cm, and $\frac{3}{4}$ is 3 times as much, so

   3×4.5 cm = 13.5 cm.

2. Reductions must be close to and a little less than reducing to 42%.

   Here is one strategy.

   Using **1a**, reducing the picture to 50% is too wide, but not too long.

   Reducing to 40%, I need to check only the width.

   40% of 12 cm:

   10% of 12 cm is 1.2 cm, so 40% is 4.8 cm (4×1.2 cm).

   So the width (4.8 cm) is less than 5 cm, so reducing to 40% will fit.

3. a. 5 times as big is an enlargement to 500%.

Hints and Comments

Overview

Students review the different strategies they have learned and used in this section.

Check Your Work

These problems are designed for student self-assessment. Students who have difficulties in answering the questions without help may need extra practice. This section is also useful for parents who want to help their children with their work.

Answers are provided in the Student Book. Have students discuss their answers with classmates.

Planning

After students complete Section D, you may assign appropriate activities from the Additional Practice section, located on page 37–38, as homework.

More or Less

Notes

4 Remind students that they are to find the price with tax using a single step rather than finding the tax and then adding.

More or Less

The copier they are using enlarges to only 200%. They will need to make several enlargements.

b. How can they do this? Use arrow language to describe the enlargements they might use.

4. Which multiplication calculation can you use to find the total cost of an item that has a 12% sales tax?

Salali buys the following items. (Prices do not include tax.)

Envelopes	\$2.05
A set of 12 pens	\$5.99
A birthday card	\$1.80
A magazine	\$3.95

5. Find Salali's total bill including 12% tax.

For Further Reflection

You have used percent bars, double number lines, arrow language, and multiplications to describe increases and decreases. Which one do you prefer? Why?

Assessment Pyramid

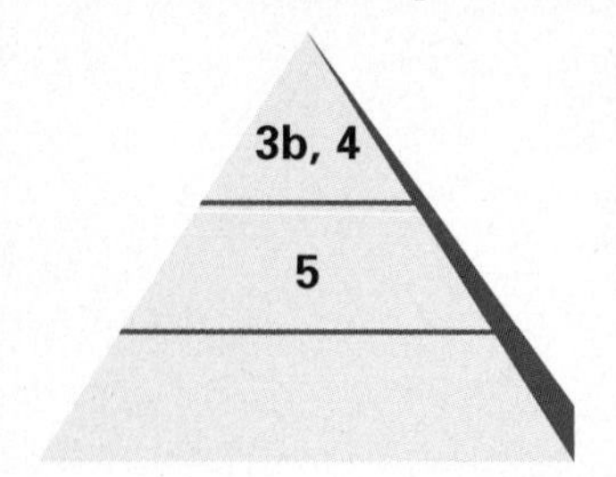

Assesses Section D goals

Reaching All Learners

Parent Involvement

For Further Reflection is a good problem for students to discuss at home.

Solutions and Samples

3. b. measurement $\xrightarrow{\times 2}$ ___ $\xrightarrow{\times 2}$ ___ $\xrightarrow{\times 1.25}$ new measurement

There are different ways to solve this problem. One way is the following.

They need to make several enlargements. Start with 200% or × 2. Then use this 200% or × 2 enlargement again. This means the result is now 400%, or × 4. This is still too small. An enlargement of the enlarged picture to 125% will result in an enlargement of the original picture to 500%.

Another way to solve this problem is to choose a measurement (for example, 100 cm) and then use the arrows to find the final amount.

$$100 \xrightarrow{\times 2} 200 \xrightarrow{\times 2} 400 \xrightarrow{\times ?} 500$$

To get from 400 to 500, you need to multiply by 1.25.

$$400 + 100 = 400 \times (1 + \tfrac{1}{4}) = 400 \times (1.25)$$

4. Multiply by 1.12.

5. Total including tax is $15.44. You can calculate the tax on each item and find the price and add all prices, but it is easier to add the prices first and calculate the tax for the total.

Total without tax is $13.79.

Including tax:

$\$13.79 \xrightarrow{\times 1.12} \$15.44$

For Further Reflection

Answers will vary according to student preferences.

From student responses to this question, you may want to create a summary of student generated pros and cons for each of these models.

Hints and Comments

Overview

Students continue completing the Check Your Work and For Further Reflections problems.

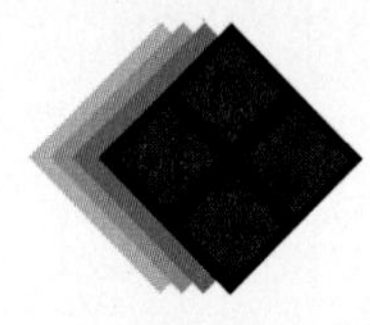

Additional Practice

Section A Produce Pricing

Red Delicious apples are priced at $2.40 per kilogram.

1. Estimate the cost of the apples.

a.

b.

Paul has $7 to spend on apples.

2. How many kilograms of Red Delicious apples can he buy?

3. Describe how to calculate the cost of the following amounts of apples, priced at $3.60 per kilogram, using a ratio table.

a. 8 kg **b.** $2\frac{1}{4}$ kg **c.** 1.6 kg

At Veggies-R-Us, customers use a special scale to find the cost of produce. It prints these receipts.

a.	b.	c.	d.
Pears	**Cucumbers**	**Red Peppers**	**Potatoes**
$2.75/kg	$2.19/kg	$4.25/kg	$0.99/kg
1.35 kg	2.86 kg	3.87 kg	0.63 kg
Total: $37125	Total: $62634	Total: $16448	Total: $62370

Unfortunately, the scale is not printing the decimal point for the total price.

4. Use estimation to determine what the total price should be on each of the receipts.

Section A. Produce Pricing

1. a. Most students will have the answer of $3.60.

If answers vary, check the strategy that is used.

Sample strategy:

- The apples on the scale weigh about $1\frac{1}{2}$ kg.

  One kilogram of Red Delicious apples costs about $2.40. One-half kilogram costs $\frac{1}{2} \times \$2.40 = \$1.20$.

  So, $1\frac{1}{2}$ kg cost $\$2.40 + \$1.20 = \$3.60$ (high estimate).

- The pointer shows 1.4 kg.
  1 kg costs about $2.40
  0.1 kg cost about $0.24
  0.2 kg cost about $0.48
  0.4 kg cost about $0.96, so
  1.4 kg cost $\$2.40 + \$0.96 = \$3.36$

b. Estimates may vary, between $6 and $7.

If students have an answer that is outside this range, check the strategy that is used.

Sample strategies:

- The apples on the scale weigh a little more than 2.5 kg and that is about 1 kg more than on the scale in a. In part a, I got $3.60, so $\$3.60 + \$2.40 = \$6.00$
- The weight is between 2.5 and 3 kg. I used a double number line to make my estimate.

$2.40	$4.80	$6	$7.20
1	2	2.5	3

The price is between $6 and $7.20, so about $6.50.

2. Paul can buy about $2\frac{9}{10}$ kg of Red Delicious apples.

Sample explanation:

Three kilograms of Red Delicious apples costs about $7.20. This is 20 cents too much. One tenth of $2.40 is 24 cents, so Paul needs to subtract $\frac{1}{10}$ kg from 3 kg, which is $2\frac{9}{10}$ kg of apples.

3. a. $28.80, sample calculation:

Cost (in dollars)	3.60	7.20	14.40	28.80
Weight (in kg)	1	2	4	8

b. $8.10, sample calculation:

Cost (in dollars)	3.60	7.20	1.80	0.90	8.10
Weight (in kg)	1	2	$\frac{1}{2}$	$\frac{1}{4}$	$2\frac{1}{4}$

c. $5.76, sample calculation:

Cost (in dollars)	3.60	.36	.72	2.16	5.76
Weight (in kg)	1	0.1	0.2	0.6	1.6

4. a. The sticker should read $3.71

Strategies will vary. Sample strategy:

The weight of the pears is about 1 kg.

One kilogram cost about $3, so $\frac{1}{3}$ kg cost about $1 and $\$3 + \$1 = \$4$.

Therefore, the decimal point should be placed between the 3 and the 7, and the number should be rounded to the nearest cent.

b. The sticker should read $6.26.

Strategies will vary. Sample strategy:

The weight of the cucumbers is a little less than 3 kg. Since 1 kg costs about $2.20, 3 kg cost about $3 \times \$2.20$ which is $6.60. Therefore, the decimal point should be placed between the 6 and the 2, and the number should be rounded to the nearest cent.

c. The sticker should read $16.45.

Strategies will vary. Sample strategy:

The weight of the red peppers is a little less than 4 kg and the price is about $4/kg.

So 4 kg cost $4 \times \$4 = \$16$

Therefore, the decimal point should be placed between the 6 and the 4, and the number should be rounded to the nearest cent.

d. The sticker should read $0.62.

Strategies will vary. Sample strategy:

The weight of the potatoes is a little more than $\frac{1}{2}$ kg.

1 kg costs about $1.00.

$\frac{1}{2}$ kg costs about $0.50, so the decimal point should be placed to the left of the 6, and the number should be rounded to the nearest cent.

Additional Practice

Section B Discounts

1. Rewrite the percents as fractions.

a. 75%
b. 10%
c. $33\frac{1}{3}\%$
d. 50%
e. $66\frac{2}{3}\%$
f. 25%

2. Rewrite the fractions as percents.

a. $\frac{3}{10}$
b. $\frac{1}{2}$
c. $\frac{1}{5}$
d. $\frac{3}{4}$
e. $\frac{8}{10}$
f. $\frac{1}{3}$

3. Describe a logical way you can solve each of the problems. Then write your answers

a. 50% of 280
b. 10% of 165
c. 20% of 500
d. 51% of 210
e. 60% of 240
f. 14% of 70

4. Seymour Sporting Goods and Sport-O-Rama are having sales. Which store has the better sale price for each item listed? Explain your choices.

Item	Seymour Sporting Goods		Sport-O-Rama	
Football	$20.00	25% off	$19.00	$4.00 off
Golf Glove	$8.40	20% off	$8.65	$1.75 off
Bowling Ball Bag	$24.95	25% off	$26.49	$8.00 off
Swimming Goggles	$5.14	30% off	$5.20	$1.50 off
Softball	$16.89	40% off	$17.00	$6.75 off
Soccer Shoes	$52.90	15% off	$50.95	$6.00 off

Section B. Discounts

1. **a.** $\frac{3}{4}$ **b.** $\frac{1}{10}$ **c.** $\frac{1}{3}$ **d.** $\frac{1}{2}$ **e.** $\frac{2}{3}$ **f.** $\frac{1}{4}$

2. **a.** 30% **b.** 50% **c.** 20% **d.** 75% **e.** 80% **f.** $33\frac{1}{3}$%

3. **a.** The answer is 140.
Strategies will vary. Sample strategy:
50% of 280 is the same as half of 280, and you can calculate that by dividing 280 by two.
$280 \div 2 = 140$

b. The answer is 16.5.
Strategies will vary. Sample strategy:
10% of 165 is the same as one one-tenth of 165, and you can calculate that by dividing 165 by ten.
$165 \div 10 = 16.5$

c. The answer is 100.
Strategies will vary. Sample strategy:
20% of 500 is the same as one fifth of 500, and you can calculate that by dividing 500 by five.
$500 \div 5 = 100$

d. The answer is 107.1, or 107.10. (Students may get this answer if they think in the context of money.)
Strategies will vary. Sample strategy:
51% is 50% plus 1%.
50% of 210 is the same as half of 210, and you can calculate that by dividing 210 by two.
$210 \div 2 = 105$
1% of 210 is the same as one hundredth of 210, and you can calculate that by dividing 210 by 100.
$210 \div 100 = 2.10$
$105 + 2.10 = 107.10$

e. The answer is 144.
Strategies will vary. Sample strategy:
60% = 50% + 10%.
50% of 240 is half of 240, which is 120.
10% of 240 is one-tenth of 240, which is 24.
So 60% of 240 is $120 + 24 = 144$.

f. The answer is 9.8.
Strategies will vary. Sample strategy:
14% = 10% + 4%.
10% of 70 is 7.
So 1% of 70 is 0.7 and 4 % is 2.8
Add the results and you get: $7 + 2.8 = 9.8$

4. **Football:**
Seymour Sporting Goods and Sport-O-Rama offer the same sale price ($15.00).
Sample explanation:
Seymour Sporting Goods is offering 25% off its regular price of $20.00, which is $\frac{1}{4}$ of $20.00, or $5.00. So the sale price is $20 – $5 = $15.
The sale price of Sport-O-Rama is
$19.00 – $4.00 = $15.00.
So, both stores have the same sale price of $15.00.

Golf Glove:
Seymour Sporting Goods has the best sale price ($6.72).
Explanations will vary. Sample explanation:
Seymour Sporting Goods is offering 20% off its regular price of $8.40, which is $\frac{1}{5}$ of $8.40.
$8.40 ÷ 5 = $1.68.
The sale price is $8.40 – $1.68 = $6.72.
The sale price of Sport-O-Rama is
$8.65 – $1.75 = $6.90.
So, Seymour Sporting Goods has a better sale price than Sport-O-Rama.

Bowling Ball Bag:
Sport-O-Rama has the best sale price ($18.49).
Explanations will vary. Sample explanation:
Seymour Sporting Goods is offering 25% off its regular price of $24.95, which is $\frac{1}{4}$ of $24.95.
$24.95÷ 4 = $6.24;
The sale price is $24.95 – $6.24 = $18.71.
The sale price of Sport-O-Rama is
$26.49 – $8.00 = $18.49.
Conclusion: Sport-O-Rama has a better sale price than Seymour Sporting Goods.

Swimming Goggles:
Seymour Sporting Goods has the best sale price ($3.60).
Explanations will vary. Sample explanation:
Seymour Sporting Goods is offering 30% off its regular price of $5.14. Thirty percent is three times ten percent.
10% of $5.14 is $0.51, so 30% of $5.14 is
3 × $0.51, which is about $1.55.
The sale price is $5.14 – $1.55, or about $3.59.
The sale price of Sport-O-Rama is
$5.20 –$1.50 = $3.70.
So, Seymour Sporting Goods has a better sale price than Sport-O-Rama.

See more Additional Practice Solutions for Section B on page 64.

Section C Many Changes

Samantha's recipe for Key lime pie was selected for a Healthy Makeover. Here is the nutritional information for both recipes.

KEY LIME PIE SERVING SIZE: ONE SLICE		NUTRITION FACTS
Nutritional Category	**Original Recipe**	**Healthful Changes**
Calories	450	One-third fewer
Fat	18 grams	Two-thirds less
Cholesterol	150 milligrams	Three-fifths less
Sodium	300 milligrams	One-quarter less
Carbohydrates	50 grams	Three-tenths more

1. Use a bar to illustrate the healthful changes in each of the five categories. Label each bar clearly.

One way to find the number of calories in one slice of the healthy recipe for Key lime pie is to multiply 450 by $\frac{2}{3}$.

2. a. What fraction can you use to calculate the new amount of fat? Amount of cholesterol? Amount of sodium? Number of grams of carbohydrates?

   b. Find the amount of each nutritional category for the healthy recipe. Explain your reasoning.

Section D More or Less

Darnel must make a poster for a presentation in his history class. He plans to enlarge a small drawing that is 28 cm by 40 cm.

1. a. How big is the poster if Darnel enlarges the drawing to 115%? 125%?

   b. Darnel enlarges the drawing to 150%. It is too small. He decides he would like to enlarge it another 150%. How large is the resulting poster?

Section C. Many Changes

1. Answers will vary. Sample response:

Calories

$\frac{1}{3}$	$\frac{1}{3}$	$\frac{1}{3}$

Fat

$\frac{1}{3}$	$\frac{1}{3}$	$\frac{1}{3}$

Cholesterol

$\frac{1}{5}$	$\frac{1}{5}$	$\frac{1}{5}$	$\frac{1}{5}$	$\frac{1}{5}$

Sodium

$\frac{1}{4}$	$\frac{1}{4}$	$\frac{1}{4}$	$\frac{1}{4}$

Carbohydrates

$\frac{1}{10}$	$\frac{1}{10}$	$\frac{1}{10}$	$\frac{1}{10}$	$\frac{1}{10}$	$\frac{1}{10}$	$\frac{1}{10}$	$\frac{1}{10}$	$\frac{1}{10}$	$\frac{1}{10}$	$\frac{1}{10}$	$\frac{1}{10}$	$\frac{1}{10}$

2. a. Fat: $\frac{1}{3}$; Cholesterol: $\frac{2}{5}$; Sodium: $\frac{3}{4}$; Carbohydrates: $1\frac{3}{10}$

b. Calories: 300

Explanations will vary. Sample student explanation:

I multiplied the number of calories in the original recipe (450) by $\frac{2}{3}$.

$450 \div 3 \times 2 = 300$ calories.

Fat: 6 g

Explanations will vary. Sample student explanation:

I multiplied the number of fat grams in the original recipe (18 g) by $\frac{1}{3}$.

$18 \times \frac{1}{3} = 18 \div 3 = 6$ g.

Cholesterol: 60 mg

Explanations will vary. Sample student explanation:

I multiplied the amount of cholesterol in the original recipe (150 mg) by $\frac{2}{5}$.

$150 \div 5 \times 2 = 60$ mg

Sodium: 225 mg

Explanations will vary. Sample student explanation:

I multiplied the amount of sodium in the original recipe (300 mg) by $\frac{3}{4}$.

$300 \div 4 \times 3 = 225$ mg

Carbohydrates: 65 g

Explanations will vary. Sample student explanations:

I multiplied the amount of carbohydrates in the original recipe (50 g) by $1\frac{3}{10}$. I know that $50 \times 1\frac{3}{10} = 50 \times 1.3 = 65$ g.

I calculated one-tenth of the amount of carbohydrates in the original recipe (50 g), which is 5 g. Then I multiplied that by three to get three-tenths, which is 15 g. Then I added this to the amount of carbohydrates in the original recipe:

$50 + 15 = 65$ g

Section D. More or Less

1. a. 32.2 cm by 46 cm

Sample explanation:

I used the following arrow string for my calculations:

original length $\xrightarrow{\times 1.15}$ enlarged length

35 cm by 50 cm

Sample explanation:

I used the following arrow string for my calculations:

original length $\xrightarrow{\times 1.25}$ enlarged length

b. 63 cm by 90 cm

Sample explanation:

I used the following arrow strings for my calculations:

original length $\xrightarrow{\times 1.5}$ ____ $\xrightarrow{\times 1.5}$ enlarged length

Additional Practice

During his presentation, Darnel plans to hand out two pictures. The pictures are both 21 cm by 27 cm. The photocopier can reduce pictures only to 75%, 70%, or 60%.

2. Explain what Darnel can do to reduce his two pictures so they both fit onto one sheet of paper that is 21.5 cm by 28 cm and the pictures are as large as possible.

Laura's grandparents started a college fund for her on her twelfth birthday. They put $500 in a savings account that earns 4% interest every year.

3. a. How much is in the account after one year? What percent of the original amount is this?

b. When Laura enters college in six years, how much money will she have in her account?

Section D. More or Less (continued)

2. Explanations will vary.

Sample explanation:

Both pictures have to fit on the paper with dimensions 21.5 cm and 28 cm. The dimensions of a picture are 21 cm by 27 cm, and that is almost the same as the paper dimensions.

So if Darnel reduces the pictures to about 50%, both pictures will fit.

original length $\xrightarrow{\times 0.75}$ ___ $\xrightarrow{\times 0.75}$ reduced length

is the same as

original length $\xrightarrow{\times 0.56}$ reduced length

This is a reduction of 56%, and that is not small enough.

original length $\xrightarrow{\times 0.70}$ ___ $\xrightarrow{\times 0.70}$ reduced length

is the same as

original length $\xrightarrow{\times 0.49}$ reduced length

This is a reduction of 49%, and that is OK.

Note that a reduction of 75% and 70% results in a reduction of about 53%.

A reduction of 75% and 60% results in a reduction of 45%.

3. a. There is $520.00 in the account after one year. This represents 104% of the original amount.

b. $632.66

Sample strategy:

I used my calculator to calculate

$500 $\xrightarrow{\times 1.04}$ ___ $\xrightarrow{\times 1.04}$ ___ $\xrightarrow{\times 1.04}$ ___

$\xrightarrow{\times 1.04}$ ___ $\xrightarrow{\times 1.04}$ ___ $\xrightarrow{\times 1.04}$ ___

Assessment Overview

Unit assessments in *Mathematics in Context* include two quizzes and a unit test. Quiz 1 is to be used anytime after students have completed Section C. Quiz 2 can be used after students have completed Section D. The Unit Test addresses all of the major goals of the unit. You can evaluate student responses to these assessments to determine what each student knows about the content goals addressed in this unit.

Pacing

Each quiz is designed to take approximately 25 minutes to complete. The Unit Test was designed to be completed during a 45-minute class period. For more information on how to use these assessments, see the Planning Assessment section on the next page.

Goal	Assessment Opportunities	Problem Levels
• Use estimation strategies to multiply fractions and decimals.	Quiz 1 Problems 1ad Test Problems 2ab	Level I
• Use number sense to multiply two decimal numbers.	Quiz 1 Problem 1bc Quiz 2 Problems 1ab Test Problems 2ab	Level I
• Find a percent number.	Quiz 1 Problem 2c Quiz 2 Problems 1b, 3c Test Problem 3a	Level I
• Calculate discount and sale price.	Quiz 1 Problems 3ab Quiz 2 Problems 1b, 3c Test Problems 1, 3b	Level I
• Know and use benchmark percents.	Quiz 1 Problems 2abc, 3ab Quiz 2 Problems 2, 3ab Test Problems 3abc	Level I
• Relate percents to fractions and decimals.	Quiz 1 Problems 2abc Quiz 2 Problems 2, 3a	Level II
• Find an original price using the sale price and the percent discount.	Test Problems 5ab	Level II
• Develop number sense.	Quiz 1 Problem 3b Quiz 2 Problem 1a Test Problems 3c, 5b	Level II
• Explore multiplicative increase and decrease (e.g., compound interest)	Test Problem 4	Level III

About the Mathematics

These assessment activities assess the major goals of the *More or Less* unit. Refer to the Goal and Assessment Opportunities section on the previous page for information regarding the goals that are assessed in each problem. Some of the problems that involve multiple skills and processes address more than one unit goal. To assess students' ability to engage in non-routine problem solving (a Level III goal in the Assessment Pyramid), some problems assess students' ability to use their skills and conceptual knowledge in new situations. For example, in the photocopier problem on the Unit Test (Problem 4), students must demonstrate their ability to apply multiplicative increase to resize a picture.

Planning Assessment

These assessments are designed for individual assessment, however some problems can be dome in pairs or small groups. It is important that students work individually if you want to evaluate each student's understanding and abilities.

Make sure you allow enough time for students to complete the problems. If students need more than one class sessions to complete the problems, it is suggested that they finish during the next mathematics class or you may assign select problems as a take-home activity. Students should be free to solve the problems their own way. Student use of calculators is at the teacher's discretion.

If individual students have difficulties with any particular problems, you may give the student the option of making a second attempt after providing him or her a hint. You may also decide to use one of the optional problems or Extension activities not previously done in class as additional assessments for students who need additional help.

Scoring

Solution and scoring guides are included for each Quiz and the Unit Test. The method of scoring depends on the types of questions on each assessment. A holistic scoring approach could also be used to evaluate an entire quiz.

Several problems require students to explain their reasoning or justify their answers. For these questions, the reasoning used by students in solving the problems as well as the correctness of the answers should be considered in your scoring and grading scheme.

Student progress toward goals of the unit should be considered when reviewing student work. Descriptive statements and specific feedback are often more informative to students than a total score or grade. You might choose to record descriptive statements of select aspects of student work as evidence of student progress toward specific goals of the unit that you have identified as essential.

Name ______________________ Date ______________

More or Less Quiz 1

Use additional paper as needed.

1. Cherries are $4.80 per kilogram.

a. Estimate the costs of the cherries on the scale.

b. Lana has $6. How many kilograms of cherries can she buy?

Gabriel used a broken calculator to find the total price of his bag of cherries. The display on the broken calculator read 7275. He remembered that the weight of his cherries was more than the weight of Lana's cherries but less than 2 kg.

c. Where do you think the decimal point should be placed? Explain your reasoning.

d. Estimate the weight of Gabriel's cherries.

2. Complete these calculations mentally. For each calculation describe your solution strategy.

a. $\frac{1}{3}$ of $120 **b.** 0.25 × $120 **c.** 40% of $120

3. In supermarket Adver, you can choose your own discount on the fruits:

Apples	**Peaches**
Regular price: $2.25 per kg	Regular price: $3.64 per kg
Today:	**Today:**
10% discount or **$0.50 off total**	**15% discount** or **$0.50 off total**

Dmitri wants to buy 1.5 kg of apples and 1 kg of peaches. He would like to have the best discount for both.

a. What should he choose for the apples: a 10% discount, or $0.50 off? Explain your reasoning.

b. What discount should he choose for the peaches? Explain your reasoning.

Name ______________________ Date ______________

More or Less Quiz 2

Use additional paper as needed.

Qual-A-Tee Supermarket changed the prices of some items in the store.

Product	Old Price	Change in Price
Butter	\$2.50	$-\frac{1}{5}$
Roasting pan	\$18	+ 10%
Bacon	\$4.50	– 40%

1. a. Make a bar to show the change in price for each item. Label the bars.

b. Calculate the new price for each item. Show your work.

2. Copy the table and fill in the correct fractions, decimals, and percents.

Fraction	Decimal	Percent
	0.5	
		10%
$1\frac{1}{5}$		
	0.20	
$\frac{7}{10}$		
		3%

A jewelry store is having a spring sale. The salesperson needs to calculate the sale prices of some of the merchandise in the store.

3. a. What fraction and percent of the original price do customers have to pay for the necklace?

b. What can the salesperson multiply to find the sale price for the necklace?

c. Compute the new price for the necklace.

Name ______________________ Date ______________

More or Less Unit Test

Use additional paper as needed.

1. Calculate the sale price of this watch.
Describe your strategy for finding the sale price.

Ace Supermarket sells pears for $1.68 per kilogram.

2. Estimate the prices for each amount of pears.
Explain how you made your estimation.

a. 2.75 kg **b.** 0.19 kg

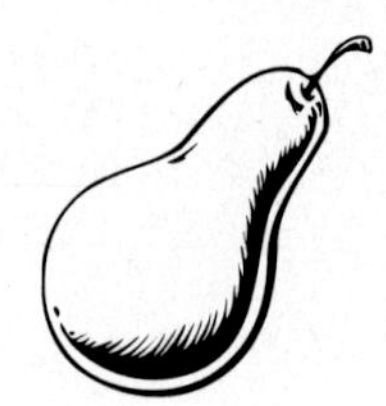

Today Acme Supermarket has a special offer for oranges.

Oranges

$4/kg

Choose your discount:

5% or **$0.50 discount**

3. a. Nikki buys 1 kg of oranges. She wants to choose the better discount. Which discount should she choose, and why?

b. Pablo buys 1.5 kg of oranges. He chooses the 5% discount. Calculate his discount.

c. For what price does it not make any difference what discount you choose? Explain.

A photocopier is to be used to enlarge this picture so that it fits in the larger frame.

4. To what percent should the picture be enlarged? Explain your answer.

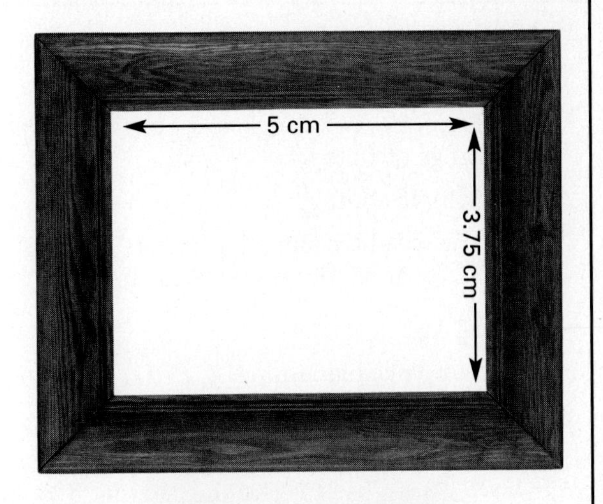

5. a. Describe how you can find the original price if you know that the sale price is $60 and the original price was increased by 50%.

b. Find the original price.

More or Less Quiz 1 Solution and Scoring Guide

Possible student answer	Suggested number of score points	Problem level
1. a. Estimates will vary. Accept estimates in the range of \$3 to \$4.00. Sample strategy: The weight is almost $\frac{3}{4}$ kg. So $\frac{1}{4}$ of \$4.80 is \$1.20, and 3 times that is \$3.60.	**1**	I
b. $1\frac{1}{4}$ kg Sample explanation: One kilogram cost \$4.80, so she has \$6 − \$4.80 = \$1.20 left. \$1.20 is $\frac{1}{4}$ of \$4.80, so she can buy $\frac{1}{4}$ kg more.	**1** (answer) **2** (explanation)	I/II
c. Between the seven and the two, so \$7.275 Sample explanation: Since Gabriel is buying more than Lana, it can't be 0.7275. Since he is buying less than 2 kg, it cannot be \$72.75.	**1** (answer) **2** (reasoning)	I
d. About 1.5 kg	**1**	I
2. a. \$40 Sample strategy: \$120 ÷ 3 = \$40	**1** (answer) **1** (reasoning)	I/II
b. \$30 Sample strategy: 0.25 × is the same as $\frac{1}{4}$ of \$120. \$120 ÷ 4 = \$30.	**1** (answer) **1** (reasoning)	I/II
c. \$48 Sample strategies: • 40% = 4 × 10% 10% of \$120 is \$12, so the answer is 4 × \$12 = \$48. • 40% = 50% − 10% 50% of \$120 is \$60 and 10% of \$120 is \$12. So the answer is \$60 − \$12 = \$48. • 40% of \$120 is the same as $\frac{2}{5}$ of \$120. \$120 ÷ 5 = \$24, so the answer is 2 × \$24 = \$48.	**1** (answer) **1** (reasoning)	I/II

Possible student answer	Suggested number of score points	Problem level
3. a. $0.50. Sample explanation: 10% of $2.25 is about $0.23, and this is less discount than $0.50.	**1** (answer) **2** (explanation)	**I**
b. 15%. Sample explanation: 10% of $3.64 is about $0.36 5% of $3.64 is about $0.18 So 15% of $3.64 is about $0.36 + $0.18, which is $0.54, and this is more than $0.50.	**1** (answer) **2** (explanation)	**I/II**
Total score points	**20**	

More or Less Quiz 2
Solution and Scoring Guide

<table>
<tr><th>Possible student answer</th><th>Suggested number of score points</th><th>Problem level</th></tr>
<tr><td>

1. a. Drawings and labels may vary.

Sample responses:

Butter

<table><tr><td>$\frac{1}{5}$</td><td>$\frac{1}{5}$</td><td>$\frac{1}{5}$</td><td>$\frac{1}{5}$</td><td>$\frac{1}{5}$</td></tr></table>

Roasting pan

<table><tr><td>100%</td><td>$\frac{1}{10}$</td></tr></table>

Bacon

<table><tr><td>60%</td><td>40%</td></tr></table>

</td><td>3</td><td>I/II</td></tr>
<tr><td>

b. Butter: $2.00

Strategies may vary. Sample strategy:

$\frac{1}{5}$ of \$2.50 is \$0.50, and \$2.50 − \$0.50 = \$2.00

Roasting pan: $19.80

Strategies may vary. Sample strategy:

10% of \$18 is one-tenth of \$18, which is \$1.80

\$18 + \$1.80 = \$19.80.

Bacon: $2.70

The new price is 60% of the old price, or $\frac{3}{5}$ of \$4.50.

$\frac{1}{5}$ of \$4.50 = \$0.90, so $\frac{3}{5}$ is 3 × \$0.90 = \$2.70

</td><td>6</td><td>I</td></tr>
<tr><td>

2.

<table>
<tr><th>Fraction</th><th>Decimal</th><th>Percent</th></tr>
<tr><td>$\frac{1}{2}$</td><td>0.5</td><td>50%</td></tr>
<tr><td>$\frac{1}{10}$</td><td>0.1</td><td>10%</td></tr>
<tr><td>$1\frac{1}{5}$</td><td>1.2</td><td>120%</td></tr>
<tr><td>$\frac{1}{5}$</td><td>0.20</td><td>20%</td></tr>
<tr><td>$\frac{7}{10}$</td><td>0.7</td><td>70%</td></tr>
<tr><td>$\frac{3}{100}$</td><td>0.03</td><td>3%</td></tr>
</table>

</td><td>6</td><td>I/II</td></tr>
</table>

Possible student answer	Suggested number of score points	Problem level
3. a. $\frac{3}{4}$ and 75%	1	I/II
b. \$360 × $\frac{3}{4}$, or \$360 × 0.75	2	I
c. \$360 × 0.75 = \$270	2	I
Total score points	20	

More or Less Unit Test Solution and Scoring Guide

Possible student answer	Suggested number of score points	Problem level
1. The sale price of the watch is \$68. Sample strategies: • Using fractions: A 20% discount is $\frac{1}{5}$ off the price. $\frac{1}{5}$ of \$85 is \$85 ÷ 5 = \$17, so the sale price is \$85 − \$17 = \$68. • Some students may use arrow language and a calculator. Sample student response: A 20% discount means the sale price is 80% of the original price. \$85 $\xrightarrow{\times \$0.8}$ Sale price So \$85 × 0.8 = \$68.	1 (answer) 1 (explanation)	I
2. a. Estimates will vary but should be between \$4.00 and \$5.00. Sample strategy: Round 2.75 kg up to 3 kg and \$1.68 down to \$1.50; 3 × \$1.50 = \$4.50. **b.** Estimates will vary but should be between \$0.30 and \$0.40. Sample strategy: Since 0.19 kg is about 0.2 kg, and \$1.68 is about \$1.70, multiply 0.2 × \$1.70. 0.2 × \$1.70 = \$0.34	**a.** 1 (answer) 2 (explanation) **b.** 1 (answer) 2 (explanation)	**a.** I **b.** I
3. a. She will choose for \$0.50. Sample explanation: 5% of \$4 is \$0.20; this is less than \$0.50, so she will choose for \$0.50. **b.** The discount is \$0.30. Sample strategy: 1.5 kg of oranges will cost \$6; 5% of \$6 is \$0.30. **c.** \$10 Strategies may vary. Sample strategy: • This means that 5% of the price is \$0.50, so 10% is \$1.00 and 100% is \$10.00. • The discount part fits 20 times in the whole bar. 5% [bar diagram] \$0.50 So to find the price I multiply \$0.50 by 20. 20 × \$0.20 = \$10.00	**a.** 1 (answer) 1 (explanation) **b.** 1 (answer) 1 (explanation) **c.** 1 (answer) 1 (explanation)	**a.** I **b.** I **c.** I/II

Possible student answer	Suggested number of score points	Problem level
4. To 125% Sample strategies: • Students may measure the dimensions of the frame (3.75 cm by 5 cm) and picture (3 cm by 4 cm) and use a ratio table. 4 cm | 1 cm | 5 cm 100% | 25% | 125% • Students may use the picture (as a kind of bar). $\frac{1}{4}$ $\frac{1}{4}$ $\frac{1}{4}$ $\frac{1}{4}$ original length $\xrightarrow{\times 1\frac{1}{4}}$ enlarged length original length $\xrightarrow{\times \$1.25}$ enlarged length So you have to enlarge the picture to 125%.	**1** (answer) **2** (explanation)	**III**
5. a. The original price was $40. **b.** Explanations may vary. Sample explanation. This bar shows an increase of 50%: original price 100% | 50% $60 I can see from the bar that to find the original price I have to find $\frac{2}{3}$ of $60. $\frac{1}{3}$ of $60 is $20, so the original price was 2 × $20 = $40.	**1** (answer) **2** (explanation)	**II** **II**
Total score points	**20**	

Glossary

The glossary defines all vocabulary words indicated in this unit. It includes the mathematical terms that may be new to students, as well as words having to do with the contexts introduced in the unit. (Note: The Student Book has no Glossary. Instead, students are encouraged to construct their own definitions, based on their personal experiences with the unit activities.)

The definitions below are specific for the use of the terms in this unit. The page numbers given are from the Student Books.

arrow language (p. 5) a way of writing calculations by showing each operation with an arrow

arrow string (p. 27) an operation written with an arrow

bar chart (p. 12) a rectangle that can be used to represent parts of a whole, such as with percents

benchmark fraction (p. 13) a fraction that is easily found, such as $\frac{1}{2}, \frac{1}{3}, \frac{1}{4}, \frac{1}{5}, \frac{1}{10}, \frac{3}{4}$

discount (p. 13) the amount that a price is reduced

double number line (p. 3) a number line with two scales, such as weight and dollars, that are proportional

estimate (p. 1) To reason about and find an answer that is close to the exact answer

interest (p. 31) earnings on an investment; a percentage of the amount invested and earned over time

percent (p. 11) for every one hundred

percent bar (p. 18) a tool for computing percentages of a number that includes visual support

pie chart (p. 11) a circular chart with sections that represent percentages or fractions for various categories of data

profits (p. 20) the amount of money earned after subtracting expenses

ratio table (p. 3) a tool for computing multiplying, dividing, or proportions using equal ratios

reduce (to a given percentage) (p. 27) for example, a length is reduced "to" 80% means the that the length is 80% of it original length

regular price (p. 15) the amount the customer pays without any discounts

sales tax (p. 29) added to the sale of goods and services, calculated as a percentage of the purchase price

segmented bar (p. 11) a bar divided into equal parts, used to compare data and make pie charts

wholesale price (p. 15) the amount the item costs the store

BRITANNICA

Mathematics in Context

Blackline Masters

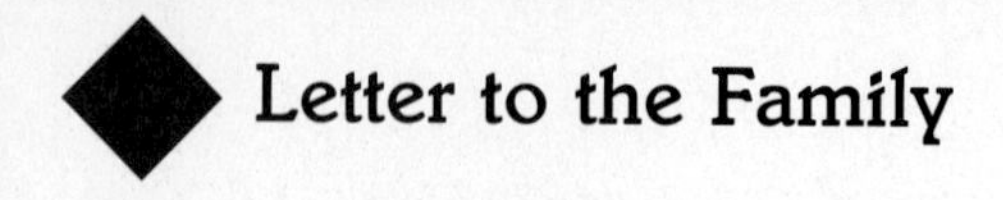

Letter to the Family

Dear Family,

Your child is about to begin working on the *Mathematics in Context* unit *More or Less*. Below is a letter to your child, describing the unit and its goals.

You can help your child relate the class work to daily life by talking about how you encounter fractions, decimals, and percents nearly every day. For instance, you might use department store ads in the newspaper to help your child figure the discount amount or discount percent offered on various sale items. Discuss your local sales tax rate with your child, and ask him or her to show how your sales tax rate can be expressed as a fraction or decimal. While dining in a restaurant, you might have your child estimate the tax on the bill. You could also give your child a store sales receipt, with the sales tax amount and total removed, and ask your child to estimate and compute the sales tax and the total bill.

To relate percent increase and decrease to daily life, your might compare prices of common items, such as bicycles, food items, or bus fares, with prices of the same items when you were your child's age. You can then ask your child to calculate the percent increase (or decrease) for each item.

We hope you enjoy helping your child investigate how fractions, decimals, and percents are used in many situations.

Sincerely,

The Mathematics in Context Development Team

Dear Student,

This unit is about the ways in which fractions, decimals, and percents are related.

Do you purchase items that need to be weighed? How is the final price determined? Calculating per unit prices and total prices requires multiplication with fraction and decimal numbers.

Do you buy your favorite items on sale? Next time you shop, notice the sale discount. Sale discounts are usually expressed in percents.

In this unit, you will use fractions and percents to find sale prices. You can use models like a double number line, a percent bar, or a ratio table to help you make calculations.

You will investigate the percent by which a photograph increases or decreases in size when you enlarge or reduce it on a photocopier.

You will also use fractions and percents to describe survey results.

While working on this unit, look for ads that list discounts in percents and newspaper articles that give survey results. Share what you find with the class.

All the situations in this unit will help you perfect your operations with fractions, decimals, and percents. Good luck.

Sincerely,

The Mathematics in Context Development Team

Name ____________________

2. a. Display the results using the segmented bar and pie chart.

b. Describe the results of the survey using fractions.

c. Describe the results of the survey using percents.

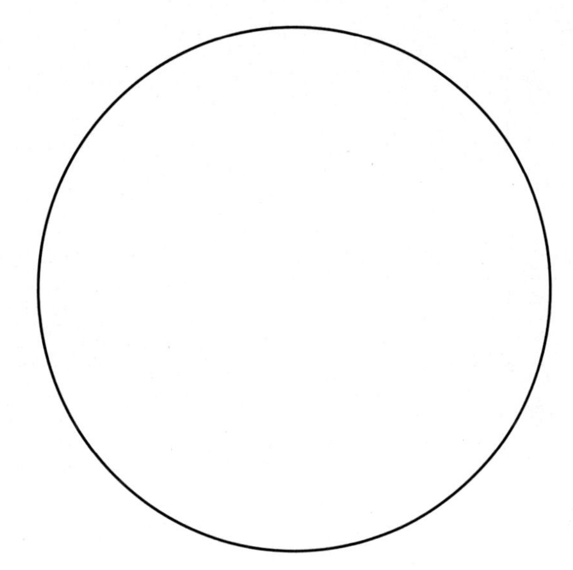

Student Activity Sheet 2

Name ____________________

Use with *More or Less*, page 14.

12. a. For each item in the table, determine whether the percent discount or cash discount gives the lower sale price.

Mark your choice in the table and give an explanation for it.

b. Add two of your own items to the table on the activity sheet.

Include the regular prices, two types of discounts, your choice, and an explanation.

If you need more room to write your explanations, you can use the back of this page.

Item	Regular Price	Sale Price	Explanation
In-line Skates	$55.00	☐ 30% off ☐ $10.00 off	
Jeans	$23.75	☐ 20% off ☐ $5.00 off	
Cell Phone	$75.00	☐ 25% off ☐ $17.50 off	
Baseball Cap	$19.95	☐ 15% off ☐ $3.50 off	
Sneakers	$45.95	☐ 20% off ☐ $9.00 off	
Earrings	$9.95	☐ 40% off ☐ $3.50 off	

Name ________________________________

7. b. Use the bars to indicate the change in profit for each department. Label the bars so that anyone can understand them.

Department	Bar
Health and Beauty	
Dairy	
Produce	
Bakery	
Meat	
Deli	

Student Activity Sheet 4

Use with *More or Less*, page 21.

Name ____________________

11. Connect the fractions and decimals that express the same number.

1.5	0.3	$\frac{1}{5}$	$\frac{1}{4}$		
$\frac{3}{4}$	0.4	$\frac{3}{100}$	0.75		
0.25	1.25	$\frac{4}{10}$	0.03		
$1\frac{1}{2}$	$\frac{3}{10}$	$\frac{25}{100}$	0.2	$1\frac{1}{4}$	$\frac{2}{5}$

Name ______________________________

Student Activity Sheet 5
Use with *More or Less*, page 22

13. Fill in the columns labeled New Price and New Price as Percentage of Old Price.

Product	Old Price	Change	New Price	New Price as Percentage of Old Price
Whole Milk	$2.10	−10%		90%
 Frozen Dinner	$4.68	−25%		
 Roasted Turkey	$13.25	+25%		
 6 Cans of Juice	$2.98	−5%		
 Canned Salmon	$3.60	+15%		

Produce Pricing

Hints and Comments

(continued from page 4T)

Materials

overhead projector, optional (one per class)

Overview

Students read scales and estimate the costs of different weights of apples. Students estimate the costs for two types of apples that sell for different prices per kilogram. They also estimate the total weight of apples one can buy for given amounts of money.

When Carol is finished with the scale, Pam weighs 10 apples she selected. This scale shows the weight of Pam's apples.

6. Estimate what Pam will pay for her apples.

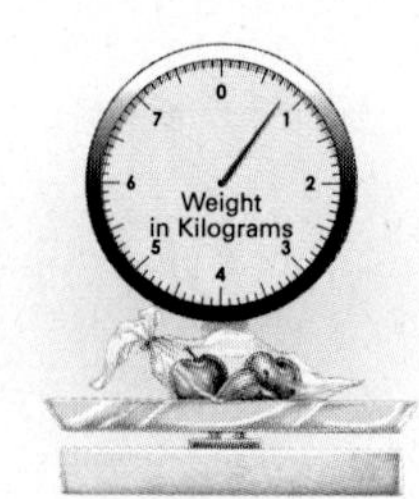

This scale shows the weight of Lia's apples.

7. Estimate what Lia will pay for her apples.

Pablo places his apples on the scale.

8. a. Suppose the weight of his apples is 2.1 kg. Copy the scale's dial and draw the pointer so it represents the weight of Pablo's apples.

b. What will Pablo pay for 2.1 kg of apples?

Save Supermarket sells several kinds of apples, including Red Delicious and Granny Smith.

Suppose Carol, Pablo, and Pam bought the same weight of Granny Smith apples instead of Red Delicious apples.

9. Using the scale weights from problems 6–8, estimate the price each person will pay for the same weight of Granny Smith apples.

10. Pam wants to buy additional apples. She has $8. Estimate the total weight of Red Delicious apples Pam can buy.

11. Pablo has $2.50 to spend on Granny Smith apples. Estimate the total weight of apples Pablo can buy.

Planning

Students may work on problems 6-8 in pairs or in small groups. Discuss the various strategies students used to solve these problems before they continue. You may want students to work on problems 9-11 individually. As students work, observe the strategies they use, especially for problem 10. Discuss students' strategies used for problems 10 and 11.

Comments About the Solutions

6. Some students may need to be reminded that 1kg of apples still costs $2.40. Students may use information from previous problems to solve these problems; for example, $\frac{1}{2}$ kg costs $1.20, and $\frac{1}{2}$ of $\frac{1}{2}$, or $\frac{1}{4}$ kg, costs $0.60.

8. If students do not know how to take one-tenth of an amount, you may suggest that they change dollars into cents, so $\frac{1}{10}$ of $2.40 is the same as $\frac{1}{10}$ of 240 cents which is 24 cents or $0.24.

9. Note that these problems introduce different kinds of apples, so different prices per kilogram are involved, which may bring about new strategies. Students' solutions will show their choice of strategies. To assess whether students know more than one of the methods discussed in this section, you might ask them to find an estimate using a different method.

10. If students are having difficulty, you can suggest that making and using a ratio table could be helpful to solve the problem. The next hint could be: Try to multiply so that you do not have any decimal numbers in the table. Have one student show his or her strategy to this problem on the overhead projector or chalkboard. If a sound strategy was used, ask students to see if that same strategy can be used to find the total weight of Granny Smith apples that Pam can buy for $8.00. Be sure to discuss the second strategy mentioned in the Solutions column. Be careful not to stress any specific algorithm.

Paul has $7 to spend on apples.

2. How many kilograms of Gala apples can he buy?

The price of Golden Delicious apples is $3.60 per kilogram.

3. Describe how you would calculate the cost of each of these amounts of apples without using a calculator.

   a. 3 kg b. 0.3 kg c. 2.3 kg

4. a. Describe how to determine $\frac{1}{2} \times \$47.00$ without using a calculator.

   b. Describe how to determine $1\frac{1}{4} \times \$8.20$ without using a calculator.

Kenji used his calculator at home to calculate 12.54 × 0.39. He wrote the answer 48906 in his notebook. It wasn't until he was at school that he discovered he had forgotten to write the decimal point in his answer. He found where the decimal point should be by estimating the answer.

5. Explain what Kenji did. Place the decimal point in his answer.

For Further Reflection

Here is a multiplication problem and the correct answer, without the decimal point:

$$568 \times 356 = 202208$$

Put a decimal point in either 568, 356, or both numbers so that you will get a new multiplication problem. Be sure that your answer for the new problem is correct!

Create at least four more problems using this method.

Hints and Comments
(continued from page 10T)

Extension

Ask each student to write three new problems about multiplying fractions and decimals like in problem 4. Then ask them to exchange papers with another student to solve the problems. After they have finished solving, have them return the papers to the writer of the problem to check the solutions.

B Discounts

Hints and Comments (continued from page 17T)

(continued from page 17T)

Materials

calculators, optional (one per student)

Check Your Work

These problems are designed for student self-assessment Answers are provided in the Student Book. Have students discuss their answers with classmates.

Overview

Students solve a discount problem in which they determine which discount gives the lowest sale price. Given the discount rate, students calculate the amount of discount and the sale price of merchandise.

Check Your Work

Dale is having a sale on small fans that regularly cost $5.98 each. Customers can choose from these three discounts.

Discount 1: 5% off   Discount 2: $0.50 off

Discount 3: $\frac{1}{5}$ off

1. Which discount gives the lowest sale price? Explain your reasoning.

Dale is selling all the air conditioners in his store to make room for other merchandise. He gives his customers a huge discount of 60%.

2. Explain how you would find the discount for an air conditioner that costs $240.

Dale has three other air conditioners to sell for $280, $200, and $275.

3. How much will each one cost after the 60% discount?

Ms. Vander and Mr. Sanchez are studying a survey of 800 customers. The survey shows that 45% of the customers gave the same response. Ms. Vander and Mr. Sanchez want to know how many customers that is. They begin by using percents they can easily write as fractions.

4. How do you think Ms. Vander and Mr. Sanchez will continue? Complete their calculations.

5. Write at least two ways to calculate 25% of 900.

For Further Reflection

Look for at least three different sale items listed in a newspaper or magazine. Calculate the discount and the sale price. Rewrite the percent discount as a fraction.

Planning

After students complete Section B, you may assign appropriate activities from the Additional Practice section, located on page 36, as homework.

Comments About the Solutions

1. Note that it is not necessary to calculate the three sale prices to solve the problem. Students may compare the three discounts when each is expressed as dollar amounts, percents, fractions, or decimals.

2. Check to see whether students use percents or benchmark fractions. Observe whether students are able to express percents as decimals and use calculators to perform one-step multiplication to solve the problem.

4. Students may use one of the following strategies:
   - find 10%, 20%, 30%, 40%, and 50%, and then find 45% (which is halfway between 40% and 50%);
   - find 10%, then 20%, then 40%, and 5% (which is half of 10%) and finally add 40% and 5%;
   - find 10%, 5%, and 50% and then subtract 5% from 50%; or
   - use percent bars, double number lines, or ratio tables to calculate their answers.

5. At this point students should know that 25% of is the same as $\frac{1}{4}$ of a number and calculate 25% of a number by dividing that number by 4. In addition, that taking one-half of one-half is another way to get the same result. Students might use a calculator to check that $\frac{1}{4}$ of 900 is $\frac{1}{2}$ of $\frac{1}{2}$ of 900, or 225.

For Further Reflection

You may ask students to make a poster presentation of their work and hang their work in the classroom.

- A third method uses **arrow language**.

  Price $\xrightarrow{\times \ldots}$ Tax amount

  It helps to remember the benchmark relationships for 1%, which are $\frac{1}{100}$ and 0.01.

14. **a.** What fraction corresponds to 8%?

b. What decimal corresponds to 8%?

c. Use arrow language (and a calculator) to show how to find the sales tax (8%) for a $20 purchase.

15. Copy the chart and fill in the last two rows. Use a sales tax of 19%.

Price in Dollars	$100.00	$10.00	$1.00
Tax in Dollars			
Total Cost with Tax			

Laura wants to compute the final cost of an item with a 19% sales tax, using one multiplication calculation. She uses arrow language to show what to multiply.

Price $\xrightarrow{\times 1.19}$ Total cost with tax

16. **a.** Explain why this arrow language is correct.

b. Write the arrow string for calculating the total cost with an 8% sales tax.

As Maritza and Jamel left Save Supermarket, Jamel bought the items on the left.

17. Find Jamel's total bill, with a sales tax of 8% included.

Maritza paid $12.63 at Save Supermarket. She wonders how much of the dollar amount is tax. The sales tax is 8%.

18. **a.** How can Maritza find out using arrow language?

b. Calculate the tax Maritza paid.

Hints and Comments

(continued from page 30T)

Planning

You may have students work on problems 13–16 individually or in small groups. Problem 14 can be used as Informal Assessment. Be sure to discuss problems 15 and 16 with the whole class.

Comments About the Solutions

15. This problem is similar to problem 12, however students now will also calculate the Total cost with tax.

18. It is important that students understand the structure of this problem. Many students will make the mistake of assuming $12.63 is 100% and calculate 8% of $12.63 to compute the amount of tax. Arrow language can prevent this common error. Drawing a bar may give visual support.

You may review problem 16 of Section C, where students discovered that when you subtract 20% of the price to get the discount price and then add 20% to the discount price, you do not get the original price back.

Additional Practice Solutions

Additional Practice

Section B Discounts

1. Rewrite the percents as fractions.

a.	75%	c.	$33\frac{1}{3}\%$	e.	$66\frac{2}{3}\%$
b.	10%	d.	50%	f.	25%

2. Rewrite the fractions as percents.

a.	$\frac{3}{10}$	c.	$\frac{1}{5}$	e.	$\frac{8}{10}$
b.	$\frac{1}{2}$	d.	$\frac{3}{4}$	f.	$\frac{1}{3}$

3. Describe a logical way you can solve each of the problems. Then write your answers

a.	50% of 280	c.	20% of 500	e.	60% of 240
b.	10% of 165	d.	51% of 210	f.	14% of 70

4. Seymour Sporting Goods and Sport-O-Rama are having sales. Which store has the better sale price for each item listed? Explain your choices.

Item	Seymour Sporting Goods		Sport-O-Rama	
Football	$20.00	25% off	$19.00	$4.00 off
Golf Glove	$8.40	20% off	$8.65	$1.75 off
Bowling Ball Bag	$24.95	25% off	$26.49	$8.00 off
Swimming Goggles	$5.14	30% off	$5.20	$1.50 off
Softball	$16.89	40% off	$17.00	$6.75 off
Soccer Shoes	$52.90	15% off	$50.95	$6.00 off

Section B. Discounts
(continued from page 36T)

Softball:

Seymour Sporting Goods has the best sale price ($10.13).

Explanations will vary. Sample explanation:

Seymour Sporting Goods is offering 40% off its regular price of $16.89. Forty percent is four times 10%.

10% of $16.89 is about $1.69, so 40% of $16.89 is 4 × $16.89, which is about $6.76.

The sale price is $16.89 – $6.76 = $10.13.

The sale price of Sport-O-Rama is $17.00 – $6.75 = $10.25.

So, Seymour Sporting Goods has a better sale price than Sport-O-Rama.

Soccer Shoes:

Sport-O-Rama has the best sale price ($44.95).

Explanations will vary. Sample explanation:

Seymour Sporting Goods is offering 15% off its regular price of $52.90.

15% = 10% + 5%

10 % of $52.90 is $5.29; , so 5% of $52.90 is $2.65.

15% of $52.90 is $5.29 + $2.65, which is $7.94.

The sale price is $52.90 – $7.94 = $44.96.

The sale price of Sport-O-Rama is $50.95 – $6.00 = $44.95.

So, Sport-O-Rama has a better sale price than Seymour Sporting Goods.